P9-CSE-329

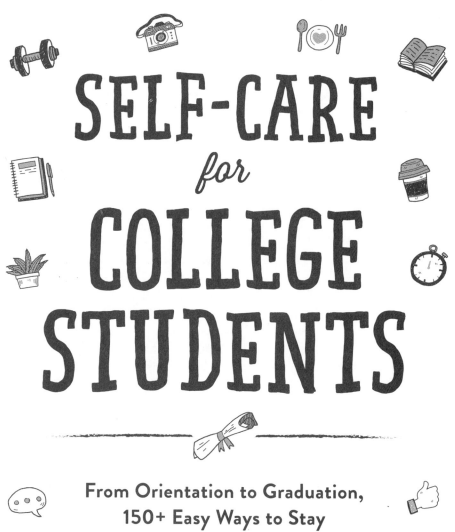

SELF-CARE
for
COLLEGE STUDENTS

From Orientation to Graduation,
150+ Easy Ways to Stay
Happy, Healthy, and Stress-Free

JULIA DELLITT

Adams Media
New York London Toronto Sydney New Delhi

Adams Media
An Imprint of Simon & Schuster, Inc.
100 Technology Center Drive
Stoughton, MA 02072

Copyright © 2019 by
Simon & Schuster, Inc.

First Adams Media
hardcover edition July 2019

ADAMS MEDIA and colophon are
trademarks of Simon & Schuster.

For information about special
discounts for bulk purchases, please
contact Simon & Schuster Special
Sales at 1-866-506-1949 or
business@simonandschuster.com.

The Simon & Schuster Speakers Bureau
can bring authors to your live event. For
more information or to book an event
contact the Simon & Schuster Speakers
Bureau at 1-866-248-3049 or visit our
website at www.simonspeakers.com.

Interior design by Julia Jacintho
Interior images © 123RF/hchjjl,
sudowoodo, puruan, huhulin,
Agnieszka Murphy, skarintut,
Dmitry Rogatnev, slothastronaut,
Ghenadie Pascari, pensiri saekoung,
Vitalii Krasnoselskyi

Manufactured in the
United States of America

3 2022

Library of Congress Cataloging-in-
Publication Data has been applied for.

ISBN 978-1-5072-1115-1
ISBN 978-1-5072-1116-8 (ebook)

DEDICATION

To my parents, Debbie and Troy, who gave
me a foundation from which to fly.

CONTENTS

INTRODUCTION – SELF-CARE 101 – 9

CHAPTER 1
BALANCE YOUR BODY: PHYSICAL SELF-CARE – 17

Drink Plenty of Water 19
Get Enough Sleep 20
Swap Processed Foods for Fresh 21
Indulge In Good Coffee or Tea..........22
Wash Your Hands 23
Sign Up for an Intramural Program ...24
Be Smart about Drugs and Alcohol ...25
Take a Power Nap 26
Eat a Meal at the Table 27
Give Yourself a Mini-Massage...........28
Take a Shower 29
Prep Healthy Snacks On the Go......30
Stand Up Straight...............................31
Cook a New Recipe............................32
Work Out at Your Fitness Center 33
Practice Sexual Safety.......................34
Wear Sunscreen.................................35
Walk to Class 36
Take Care of Your Lungs 37
Go for a Run on Campus....................38
Take Advantage of
 Wellness Programs........................39
Stretch Your Fingers 40
Rest Your Eyes....................................41
Plan Your Weekly Meals 42
Make a Doctor's Appointment 43
Stand More 44
Brush Your Teeth 45
Use Your Core Muscles 46
Relax Your Jaw 47
Enjoy Something Green 48
Skip the Snooze Button.....................49
Count Your Steps 50
Do a Little Dance...............................51
Opt for Less Sugar 52
Use a Face Mask................................53
Dress Up 54
Soak Up the Sun................................55

CHAPTER 2
BOOST YOUR BRAIN: MENTAL SELF-CARE – 57

Try the 90-Minute Sprint 59
Slow Your Scroll...............................60
Get Lost in a Book............................61
Take a Short Study Break 62
Learn a New Skill..............................63
Eliminate a Stressor 64
Listen to a Podcast 65
Put a Stop to Harmful Rumination ..66
Write Lecture Notes by Hand 67
Switch Up Your Study Scenery........68
Draw Something from Memory 69
Create a Morning Routine 70
Count Backward from Fifty 71
Do a Jigsaw Puzzle...........................72
Sing a Favorite Song 73
Break Up a Big Task..........................74
Watch a Funny Video 75
Play a Musical Instrument................76
Ask a Question 77

Get Into a State of Flow 78
Play Sudoku 79
Take a Vitamin 80
Be Vulnerable 81
Make Something with Your Hands ...82
Learn Your Burnout Signals.............83
Daydream for 15 Minutes.................84
Go Somewhere New.........................85
Squeeze a Stress Ball.......................86
Start a Journal.................................. 87
Create a Custom Playlist...................88
Visit a Museum.................................89
Clean Out Your Bag..........................90
Open the Windows 91
Leave Your Phone at Home.............. 92
Hold a 1-Minute Plank.....................93
Flip Through a Comic........................94
Snack On Fruit 95

CHAPTER 3
NOURISH YOUR SPIRIT: SPIRITUAL SELF-CARE – 97

Attend a Worship Service.................99
Contribute to a Cause 100
Listen to Soothing Music................101
Read a Spiritual Passage 102
Plan for Unstructured Time 103
Volunteer in Your Community........104
Meditate..105
Go On a Campus
    Ministry Retreat 106
Make a Gratitude List 107

Pray..108
Balance Your Chakras 109
Learn about a Different Faith 110
Celebrate the Highs *and* Lows 111
Smell an Essential Oil 112
Carve Out a Quiet Moment.............113
Read Your Tarot Cards 114
Let Go of What You Can't Control....115
Ask Your Friends about Their Beliefs...116
Focus On the Present......................117

Participate in a
Religious Student Group 118
Try a Yoga Class 119
Visit with a Spiritual Advisor 120
Talk about Vocations
with Your Peers............................121
Cozy Up 122
Create a Personal Mantra 123
Determine Your Top Three Values .. 124
Help Someone..............................125

Set an Evening Ritual.......................126
Learn about Your Faith History 127
Light a Candle............................... 128
Spend Time in Nature......................129
Promote Balance with Amethyst ... 130
Attend an Interfaith Event...............131
Try Acupuncture.............................132
Look At Your Astrology Chart 133
Care for a Plant 134
Watch the Sun Rise or Set 135

CHAPTER 4
HONOR YOUR HEART: EMOTIONAL SELF-CARE – 137

Say No......................................139
Call a Loved One............................ 140
Stay In 141
Give Yourself a Compliment 142
Ask for Help.................................. 143
Watch for Red Flags 144
Reframe Complaints 145
Enjoy Single Life............................. 146
Surround Yourself with
Positive People 147
Send a Thank-You Note................... 148
Enjoy Alone Time 149
Be Mindful of the
Comparison Trap 150
Build a Support System 151
Write Down Five Words
That Describe You 152
See a Campus Counselor 153
Set a Healthy Boundary 154
Embrace a Mistake..........................155
Identify Emotional Triggers 156

Treat Yourself 157
Distinguish Your Inner Circle 158
Do a Mental Health Screening 159
Give a Compliment 160
Linger in Nostalgia 161
Fact-Check a Thought.....................162
Cuddle an Animal............................163
Write a Letter to Your Future Self ... 164
Celebrate a Friend's Success............165
Let Go of an Old Story.....................166
Redirect Envy 167
Practice Self-Awareness.................. 168
Buy Yourself Flowers.......................169
Take a Mental Health Day............... 170
Have a Good Cry 171
Vent to Someone You Trust.............172
Cover Yourself with a
Weighted Blanket.......................173
Add Positivity to Your Morning 174
Believe In a Better Tomorrow 175

CHAPTER 5
FIND YOUR PURPOSE: PROFESSIONAL SELF-CARE – 177

Introduce Yourself to
Someone New 179

Get Rid of Clutter...........................180

Develop a Study Ritual 181

Do Something Terrifying
and Exciting 182

Get a Part-Time Job 183

Set a Realistic Goal 184

Get to Know Your Professors...........185

Plan Your Schedule
with an Advisor 186

Create a Vision Board.....................187

Take an Elective Class 188

Understand Your Student Loans
and Financial Aid 189

Join a Club 190

Make Your Space Feel Like Home... 191

Hone Your Leadership Style............192

Know the Pros and Cons
of Credit Cards...........................193

Manage a Group Project 194

Learn Hard and Soft Skills...............195

Open a Savings Account 196

Send a Cold Email 197

Explore a Study Abroad Program... 198

Job Shadow 199

Learn Basic Coding 200

Develop an Online Portfolio 201

Visit a Career Counselor 202

Try Morning Pages 203

Take a Personality Test 204

Meet with a Life Coach 205

Get a Tutor.......................................206

Write a Personal Statement 207

Attend an Extracurricular
Seminar 208

Organize Your Course Materials.... 209

Practice an Open Mind 210

Apply for an Internship.....................211

Watch a Documentary 212

Consider Switching Majors.............213

Collect Inspiring Quotes 214

Let Your Curiosity Lead You............215

INDEX – 216

INTRODUCTION
SELF-CARE 101

Take a shower. Meditate. Go for a walk. It seems like self-care is every-where: in celeb posts while scrolling through social media, online when skimming a favorite website before class. But self-care is more than just a face mask, an early bedtime, and a #treatyoself moment. It is the intentional care for your personal health. Ever heard the saying, "You can't pour from an empty cup?" Sure, it's a bit of a cliché, but it's true—and it's a great way to think about self-care. Between all of the exams, fights with roommates over who drank the last of the milk (it definitely wasn't you), and pressure to figure out what you want in life, it's easy to end up trying to pour just one last drop from that cup half the time (okay, more than half the time—let's be real). But whenever you do something for yourself—like taking a power nap before that long chem lab—you are refilling that cup (a.k.a. your physical, mental, spiritual, emotional, and professional reserves). Once restored, you can take on everything from that upcoming philosophy paper, to working up the courage to sit with someone new in the dining hall. In short, self-care is your ticket to being your best self!

Why It Matters

But how exactly are you supposed to take care of yourself when there is so much to do?! From choosing between majors and passing exams, to hanging out with friends and fitting five campus events into one week, you've got a lot going on! But self-care actually helps you make the most of it all. Instead of simply adding another to-do item to your list, self-care gives you the tools to tackle anything that comes your way.

Another great thing about self-care is that the more you do it, the more you're able to make it your own. As you try out different acts of self-care, you figure out which ones are helpful, and which ones just aren't for you; maybe breathing exercises just don't do it for you, but engaging in something creative, like sketching, does. Or maybe working out in the fitness center isn't your thing, but you really enjoy jogging around campus. You will also start to notice what parts of your life are in need of more care at any given time. For example, maybe you feel replenished physically after sleeping in before an afternoon class, but need more emotional self-care following a fight with a friend the night before. Paying attention to the type (or types) of self-care you need from one day to the next will allow you to restore and balance these different aspects of your health.

Types of Self-Care

The five main types of self-care are physical, mental, spiritual, emotional, and professional. Each type can stand on its own, but they can also work together. For example, going to the gym is obviously physical self-care, but it can also help you clear your mind (mental self-care) and let go of something that's been bugging you (emotional self-care). Ideally, you'll find activities in each category helpful, but at different points during your college career, you may find yourself needing more personal care in one or more specific types at a time. Maybe you're going through a bad breakup or the loss of a loved one and you need to give extra attention to your emotional health. Or maybe you're drowning in midterm exams, have caught that cold that your roommate brought home last week, and just really need to focus on getting yourself back in line with some mental self-care. The more you explore and try out different types of self-care, the easier it will be to figure out what your needs are at a given time and what acts work best for you!

Physical

Physical self-care focuses on how you take care of your body. And it's not *just* about working out and eating right (though that's important too). It's also about your long-term health, and how regular physical care impacts how you feel overall. Think about what happens when you're slammed by a nasty flu bug—everything else stops, right? You're sidelined until you get healthy, and you can't get healthy without rest, nourishment, and hydration. Regular physical self-care helps prevent these kind of illnesses, as well as burnout and fatigue; it's the foundation that keeps your engine running—so you can do all the things you want *and* need to do!

So when you feel like crawling under the covers and sleeping for a month, a little physical self-care can save the day! Maybe you set a regular bedtime routine so you can fall asleep at a reasonable time every night (or at least every weekday night). Or maybe you talk to an academic advisor about ways to better manage your workload so you aren't staying up until 1 a.m. finishing reports every other day. Or perhaps you take a multi-vitamin every day so your diet stays on track in light of that all-access ice cream bar in the dining hall. Caring for your body lets you perform at your best in everything that comes your way!

Mental

Mental self-care affects how you think, feel, and behave; it's how you keep your brain sharp in order to make decisions, react to a situation, and relate to other people. Mental health also spans a wide spectrum.

For some people, managing mental health might mean navigating a fight with a friend, learning how to handle stress during exams, or just finding ways to recharge the brain after a long week of classes. Maybe your roommate was upset because you didn't want to watch a movie with her the other night, and you're now trying to look at the issue from her point of view. Or maybe you're waiting to hear back from an internship you applied for, so you make fun plans with your fraternity buddies to distract yourself until you get the call.

For others, mental self-care might mean dealing with treatment for or recovery from a diagnosed mental illness or disorder, such as attention deficit disorder, anxiety, depression, or bipolar disorder. If treatment or recovery is needed, receiving care from a trained health professional—on top of practicing regular self-care—is key.

Spiritual

Spiritual self-care is different for everyone, but ultimately it focuses on how you connect to the ethereal realm. You might be part of an organized religion or faith tradition, or you may be building on a personal sense of connection to a higher power, the universe, etc. You may be interested in certain sacred texts, liturgies, or prayers, or something as simple as a gratitude list. Perhaps you set aside 15 minutes every morning for a short self-reflection before heading off to class—or you attend a campus service every weekend. You might sign up for a religious studies class even if your major is completely different, or practice a 5-minute meditation to clear and refocus your mind during a stressful situation. There are many paths to finding deeper meaning, and spiritual self-care is how you explore and nurture the right path(s) for you.

Emotional

Emotional self-care focuses on your ability to express yourself. It teaches you how to tune into your emotions, explore how these emotions might impact your actions, and express them in healthy ways. Maybe you simply decide not to answer the phone when your dad calls because you aren't in the mood to chat and just need some time alone with your feelings. Or maybe you set better boundaries with a high school bestie who has been demanding a lot of your time lately. It's how you replenish your emotional "cup" in order to sustain healthy relationships—both with yourself and with others. For you, it might mean signing up for a campus therapy appointment even when you're not sure what's "wrong," or venting to a trusted friend about a negative thought you can't let go of. Making sure you have what you need to thrive emotionally is essential (both during and beyond college), and practicing this kind of self-care will be key.

Professional

Professional self-care is kind of a catchall for everything you do related to your career and/or academics. From work-studies to class presentations, there are all kinds of obligations to juggle, and professional self-care helps you balance them. Through acts of professional self-care, you can bump up any lower grades that might have you worrying about your GPA (grade point average); broaden your horizons by taking classes outside your comfort zone; and set realistic goals for how you manage your time, money, and energy at school, work, and your dorm.

Professional self-care is how you learn to adjust to information overload, multitask without getting overwhelmed, beat that urge to procrastinate, and make sure you don't overextend yourself. It also helps you on your journey to discover what your unique skills are and what makes you happy. Maybe you always planned to be a lawyer, but then you signed up for an art history class and now realize that this is the best path for you. Or maybe you volunteer with a campus events group and discover you're great at ticket sales and staff management.

With this knowledge, you can not only succeed in your own life, but also make a difference in the world around you! Your love of interior design and degree in architecture could result in a career building homes for families in need, for example. Or all that work pushing yourself in microbiology classes gets you into medical school and on track to becoming a doctor. The sky's the limit!

What Self-Care Isn't

Just as there is no one-size-fits-all type of self-care, there is also no one "right" way to approach it; it can mean just about anything you want it to. Self-care for you could mean going shopping with your roommate for a little retail therapy after a tough test, or taking a nice long walk around campus between classes. It might involve some pricier products, or be completely free. And it could take just 2 minutes before a morning lecture, or 2 hours after a club meeting in the afternoon. The main goals of self-care are to honor your needs, avoid burnout, and ultimately create routines that allow you to function as your best self. Still, it's worth noting that self-care can shift into murky, unhealthy waters if unchecked. The following are key things to look out for if you feel that your self-care practices may need to be adjusted:

- You're focusing on other people's self-care "rules," instead of what is best for you.

- You only do certain self-care activities to "keep up" with your friends (or that picture-perfect #fitspo account), such as buying an overpriced latte when you aren't really a fan of coffee, or pretending to care about a beauty treatment you have no true interest in.

- You view self-care as a free pass to do whatever you want, no matter how it might affect people around you. This includes things like skipping a big group presentation to lie in bed all day, ghosting a campus event you signed up to help out at, or constantly bailing on plans with friends.

• You use self-care to live outside your means or justify unhealthy coping mechanisms. This includes racking up credit card debt for off-campus wellness retreats; never visiting the health clinic; or using food, alcohol, or drugs to numb the pain of a breakup.

• You assume self-care will fix every problem in your life and bring total, everlasting happiness. College is full of ups and downs and twists and turns that everyone experiences—after all, these challenges are what ultimately make you grow as a person. Self-care isn't a cure-all: it is a guide and aid in your own journey through these years.

• You treat self-care as a game to win—a puzzle to perfect, or a one-time action to take—rather than an ongoing, ever-changing way of living. It involves regular, conscious effort. There's no gold star rewarded at the "end" alongside your cap and gown: your prize is an improved state of well-being.

Taking Charge of Your Self-Care

Now that you know what self-care is—and isn't—and how to distinguish between the different types of self-care, it's time to get started! You can use the following activities however you want, whether you flip to a specific chapter whenever you're in need of a little TLC in a certain area, or you read through from beginning to end.

CHAPTER 1

BALANCE YOUR BODY: PHYSICAL SELF-CARE

You get one body in this life. Ideally, you choose to embrace and cherish it, but unfortunately, it can be a little too easy to do the exact opposite as a college student. It's not that you don't care about your health; you just have so much going on in your life that physical wellness ends up falling by the wayside. (Hey, you've got places to go and people to see—and walking to class counts as cardio, right?) Luckily, physical self-care isn't "all or nothing," "either you are a workout fiend or a hopeless couch potato." No, balancing your body isn't necessarily about losing weight, getting six-pack abs, or running marathons. It's about honoring your physical needs so you can function properly and reduce your risk of things like heart disease, cancer, stroke, obesity, and diabetes. After all, your body is a sacred temple that deserves to be treated with care and respect!

This chapter offers all kinds of simple ways to care for your physical health, from power naps to a well-balanced diet to proper hygiene. You'll explore ways to move your body, bolster energy levels, care for your skin and internal organs, stretch your muscles, feed your belly, and—most importantly—feel your best.

DRINK PLENTY OF WATER

Between all of the class lectures, outings with friends, and campus-wide events, you probably reach for all kinds of drinks when you're thirsty—juice, soda, coffee, milk—but you may not always remember the most important one: water. Your body constantly loses water over the course of the day and, consequently, needs to be replenished to prevent dehydration. Staying hydrated keeps your heart healthy, supports clear skin, promotes digestion, and lifts energy and concentration levels. Plus, it's free!

Whether you're darting from class to class or staying up late to study for that chemistry exam, aim to drink at least eight 8-ounce glasses of water each day. To make it easier, carry a reusable bottle with you and keep a full glass of water next to your bed. If plain water is just too boring, you can infuse it with berries, citrus, or cucumber slices to switch things up. If you need an extra hydration lift, add water-rich fruits and veggies like oranges, strawberries, celery, and tomatoes to your diet. You can also use an app, like Plant Nanny or My Water Balance, to track your water intake, or set a regular timer on your phone as a reminder to take a sip.

GET ENOUGH SLEEP

Classmates are always bragging about sleep deprivation—"I was up until 3 a.m. this morning!"—like it's a badge of honor, but getting enough sleep helps you stay alert and improves memory. It also protects your body against viruses that typically roam college campuses from one semester to the next.

Aim for a solid 6–8 hours of sleep each night in order to wake up feeling rested and ready to take on the day. Sticking to the same schedule for going to bed and getting up in the morning will prevent a disruption to your biological clock. Also, you should view your bed as a place for sleeping only—not where you read, study, watch TV, or look at your phone. This will make falling asleep much easier. It can also help to nix caffeine after midday, and practice winding down with a relaxing bedtime routine like yoga or meditation.

SWAP PROCESSED FOODS FOR FRESH

You're constantly surrounded by delicious things to eat: drive-through burgers, vending machine snacks, and dining hall options galore. While you can definitely indulge in your favorites from time to time, you should keep an eye on processed foods that have a long ingredient list (such as cookies, chips, and frozen pizza). These items are usually made to have a long shelf life, which is great for stocking up your dorm room cabinet, but not so great for your health.

Whether you're relying on meal plan points in the cafeteria or have access to a kitchen, swap out processed foods for fresh ones whenever possible. For example, instead of boxed cereal, try a warm bowl of steel-cut oats with berries. Trade packaged pretzels for baby carrots and hummus if you need a mid-homework snack, and replace the extra cheese on your sub sandwich with lots of lettuce and tomato slices. Eating fresh, whole foods will keep you energized and prevent those awkwardly loud stomach growls during class.

INDULGE IN GOOD COFFEE OR TEA

It seems like caffeine goes hand in hand with college, and for good reason: it provides an extra jolt of energy right when you need it. However, coffee and caffeinated tea in moderation are good for more than just a midmorning pick-me-up on your way to class. Both beverages also contain antioxidants, which can assist with weight loss and fight inflammation. In addition, coffee improves endurance and memory, helps you to stay focused and alert, and protects your brain from illness. And if you prefer a cup of tea to coffee, you'll benefit from a soothed digestive system, an improved immune system, increased bone strength, and a reduced risk of heart attack or stroke.

Whichever fuel you choose, make it part of your routine in a way that feels like a little luxury. The next time you're on a coffee shop "date" with your laptop, grab a bag of your favorite coffee beans to brew at home. Warm up a mug to help you stay awake on nights when you're up late studying, or prep a batch of cold brew to serve as your motivation to get out of bed the next morning. Splurge on that oat milk or green tea latte as a reward the next time you finish a big project or essay.

WASH YOUR HANDS

Living with roommates, touching library stairwells, opening classroom doors, sharing the rec center with strangers—you're exposed to germs and bacteria constantly. That's why washing your hands is the number one thing you can do to stay healthy and avoid getting sick. Use soap and clean running water and scrub your hands for at least 30 seconds (about as long as it takes to sing the "Happy Birthday to You" song—in your head, of course). Make sure you wash your hands after using the restroom, before touching or eating food, after touching an animal, when taking the garbage out, or if you're blowing your nose, sneezing, or coughing. And if you don't have access to soap and/or clean water in the moment, you can keep an alcohol-based hand sanitizer in your bag or car as an easy way to stay germ-free.

SIGN UP FOR AN INTRAMURAL PROGRAM

Joining a team is a great way to stay active and meet new people, but sometimes your schedule is just too busy for an official sports team—or you prefer something more casual. Intramural programs are the perfect happy medium! Most schools provide women's, men's, and coed league options across a wide variety of sports, like softball, soccer, volleyball, tennis, ultimate frisbee, and basketball. These teams tend to have a smaller time commitment and more flexibility with practices and games than official college sports do. Some are still competitive in nature, while others are a bit more recreational—so you can take your pick! On an intramural team, you don't typically have to worry about being "the best" or doing "whatever it takes" to succeed: the goal is to have fun. You'll also be able take a break from schoolwork—and work off lingering frustration after a difficult class—while making great memories in the process.

BE SMART ABOUT DRUGS AND ALCOHOL

Alcohol and drug use is often seen as a rite of passage in college, but the truth is, you can have just as much fun without them. You can invite a couple of friends over to watch a show or play card games, go hiking, join a league for a random sport like bowling, or check out a local restaurant. Basically, you can do anything!

If you're of legal age and do choose to drink alcohol or experiment with legal recreational drugs, however, be sure to make informed decisions. Know your alcohol tolerance levels, your drink serving sizes, and your reasons for drinking. Do you feel like you *need* this glass of wine to get through the day/night? Or is it a treat you simply want to enjoy over takeout with friends? Always plan rides ahead of time when you know you will be drinking or using drugs; ask a sober friend to drive you, or keep your phone battery charged so you and your friends can call a car service for a ride at the end of the night. Additionally, read up on the risks and side effects involved with legal recreational drug use, and only take prescription medications per your doctor's instructions. This isn't about killing your buzz or preventing you from having a good time—it's simply about lessening the risks involved!

TAKE A POWER NAP

Picture this: it's midday after a long morning of classes. You just ate lunch, and your eyes are starting to feel heavy. You might gaze longingly toward your comfy bed and consider crashing for several hours before tackling your homework—but hold on a minute! A speedy power nap of 20–30 minutes is actually the best option. Short naps of 30 minutes or less are proven to strengthen your learning, motor, and memory skills, and can help get your body going again if that latest all-nighter has you feeling groggy.

Try to schedule a power nap between classes or before a long study session. Set your alarm for the time you need or want to wake up, and make sure the nap is at least several hours before bedtime so you don't disrupt your regular sleep. Disable notifications on your phone, or put it on airplane mode, and find a dark, quiet spot. And if thoughts keep popping up, preventing you from catching those ZZs, jot them down on a piece of paper to deal with when you wake up.

EAT A MEAL AT THE TABLE

How often do you eat "offline," or away from a screen? If the answer is "Um...not that often," you're not alone. Sinking into your couch or bed to watch a new TV show or surf your social media accounts as you eat dinner can *seem* like a great way to unwind (or multitask before prepping for exams), but eating meals at the table, sans any electronic devices, gives your body the proper time to digest and enjoy your food. When sitting down without your phone or TV present, you can better appreciate the taste and texture of the meal, and notice the bodily cues that signal when you're full. It also improves your attention span, because you're intentionally focused on doing one thing at a time. And if you can convince your roommates or Greek life cohorts to join you, it's a great way to reconnect and be present with one another!

GIVE YOURSELF A MINI-MASSAGE

Between classes, homework, and a busy social calendar, a luxurious 90-minute full-body massage may not fit into your schedule (or budget). Instead, you can opt for a quick, DIY version at home! Mini-massages are a great way to target the parts of your body most susceptible to aches, pain, and stress-induced tension (the head, neck, shoulders, lower back, feet). Taking even a few minutes to work out a knot or rub a sore area can also improve your focus in class, increase dopamine (otherwise known as the feel-good hormone), improve circulation, and help you sleep better.

When giving yourself a massage, you can use a tennis ball, a foam roller, or your hands. To start, try the following full-body technique. First, massage your temples and the bridge of your nose (between your eyes) with your thumbs and pointer fingers. Next, stretch out your wrists to improve flexibility and strength after typing on your laptop all day. Then, give yourself a hug to support your upper back, reaching for opposite shoulders to stretch the space between your shoulder blades. Finally, flex and point your feet in both directions, wiggle your toes, and massage your arches to relax pressure points.

TAKE A SHOWER

Keeping clean is a practical part of life—but it's also good for your body, and it can make you feel like a brand-new person whenever you need to reset. A morning shower jump-starts your busy day: you smell good, you feel clean and confident, and your mind is clear and alert. It is especially good for those mornings when you really struggle to drag yourself out of bed for an early class or a hike with friends (why did you agree to that again?). If you're game, turn on the cold water briefly during your shower to increase your heart rate and get the blood pumping throughout your body. It can be just the wake-up call you need! And after a long day of listening to professors or sweating through a tough workout class, a hot shower will relieve stress, soothe aches and pains, promote muscle recovery, improve circulation, help you sleep better, and even assist with sinus problems.

PREP HEALTHY SNACKS ON THE GO

Keeping up a healthy diet when your schedule is so jam-packed is challenging—and all of those snacks from the vending machine, drive-through orders, and late-night pizza deliveries add up. Whether you are racing out the door, sans breakfast, to make it to class on time, or staying late at the library to finish a report, healthy snacks can tide you over until you have time for a sit-down meal, and will also curb the junk food temptations. They can also be the perfect energy boost before an exam or after a long lecture.

Always keep a snack or two on hand wherever you go. Pick snacks based on what's filling, mostly all-natural, and ready to take on the go. Some great snacks include trail mix with nuts and dried fruit, washed and cut fresh fruit, single-serving cheese with whole grain crackers or pretzels, smoothies, low-sugar protein or granola bars, Greek yogurt, carrots and hummus, applesauce, and veggie chips. You can throw these in your backpack, purse, or the back seat of your car, or keep them in a small dorm room refrigerator, or in your desk drawer.

STAND UP STRAIGHT

Mom or Dad ever tell you to stand (or sit) up straight? As annoying as it is, they're right (not that you have to tell them that). In fact, good posture is proven to improve self-esteem, increase the amount of oxygen entering your lungs, and strengthen your spine—while reducing unnecessary pressure on your vertebrae and body muscles. Have a classic case of slumping shoulders? No worries: it's a fairly easy fix! All you need to do is start taking note of when you are slouching, then make an adjustment. Over time, it will become second nature to check in on your posture throughout the day—until it's no longer necessary.

When correcting your standing posture, think about stacking your head over your shoulders, hips over feet. If you find yourself hunched over driving or studying, pull your belly in and draw your shoulders up and back while putting both feet on the ground. And if you're looking down at your phone or tablet while sitting, bring the device forward in front of you and sit up tall to look out and up slightly. You can also ask a friend to remind you to stand and sit up straight whenever they see you slouching. There are even devices on the market (like UPRIGHT GO and the Sense-U brace) that use a sensor and smartphone app to correct bad posture!

COOK A NEW RECIPE

When you think about cooking, you probably reach for the easiest, cheapest meal: good ol' ramen noodles. But the truth is, cooking a meal without instant noodles doesn't have to be complicated or expensive. There are countless recipes out there that take less than 30 minutes to make, and use affordable ingredients you can find at the local store or borrow from roommates (with permission, of course). You can check out a cookbook from the school library, borrow a tried-and-true recipe from a friend, or search the Internet for ideas.

Trying a new recipe once in a while can help you stay motivated to eat right, foster a sense of independence, and keep your taste buds happy. You can start with some basics like overnight oats or avocado toast for breakfast, burrito bowls and Mason jar salads for lunch, and homemade energy balls for dessert or a snack—or try a revamped ramen recipe with meat, fried egg, and veggies! Stock up on rice, pasta, herbs and spices, jarred sauce, and canned beans, and choose low-cost, healthy options like eggs, inexpensive cuts of meat, frozen veggies, and fruit while shopping.

WORK OUT AT YOUR FITNESS CENTER

You already know that exercising is a key part of physical health—but the cost of a gym membership can be pretty pricey (not to mention finding the motivation to get in the car and drive there more than once a month). Fortunately, there is good news: your tuition dollars have basically already paid for access to a fitness center—and it's right on campus! The point of your fitness center is truly to support you on your health and wellness journey, so take advantage. Ask about perks like free or low-cost personal training sessions, Q&A opportunities with a registered dietitian or fitness consultant, and exercise classes. Most campus fitness centers will also offer weight lifting equipment, cardio machines, full-sized courts, running tracks, workout videos, and separate rooms for activities like yoga, aerobics, and Pilates.

Not only is exercise linked with higher GPAs in college students, but it can also help you combat that pesky Freshman 15 weight gain (even if it's your third year), build a connection with your school, and create a healthy routine that carries into your graduate life. Need to study for an exam? Bring your textbook along and review the material while using a stationary bike!

PRACTICE SEXUAL SAFETY

Sexual activity is a major topic of thought and discussion in college. Maybe your parents bring it up during a phone call, thinking they are being oh-so-casual, or a roommate asks for your advice, or you start dating someone new and it inevitably comes up. Regardless, sexual activity is entirely your choice. You can decide to abstain entirely, start being sexually active for the first time, or continue whatever feels right for you.

No matter what you choose, the most important thing to remember is to always practice safety in your decisions. This includes everything from ensuring consent on both sides, to taking appropriate measures to protect your body from sexually transmitted diseases and unwanted pregnancy. Ideally, you should plan a visit to your campus health center or a local clinic to get tested for any STDs (along with your partner!) at least twice a year. In addition, familiarize yourself with campus policies around sexual behavior and assault so you know your rights. You may also want to talk with your friends or roommates about sex so you can look out for each other and support safe choices.

WEAR SUNSCREEN

Sunscreen isn't reserved for spring break beach days or tanning on the quad. You'll want to wear it year-round to protect your skin, whether it's hot and sunny, or cool and cloudy (you'd be surprised by how much sun you can get when it's overcast!).

While premature aging is probably one of the *last* things you're thinking about in college, a lot of sun exposure happens during these years. From studying outside, to socializing at a barbecue, to playing sports on a bright autumn afternoon, you are constantly in the sun. The effects are cumulative, too, so every moment spent under the sun adds up. If you like the bronzed look, skip tanning beds in favor of self-tanner, then cover up appropriately. Wear sunglasses and a hat if you're outdoors for long periods of time, and apply broad-spectrum sunscreen to protect against UVA and UVB rays. Also be sure to reapply every couple of hours. Your college might even provide public sunscreen dispensers or sun safety kits, so take full advantage.

WALK TO CLASS

Depending on the size of your campus, you can easily walk to and from places like the dining hall, classes, the library, and the fitness center. Walking is a great way to stay active, and if you need to take several sets of stairs or fast-walk to arrive somewhere on time, you may even break a sweat—no gym required! Try to walk to classes as much as possible. You can even think of it as a way to multitask; use the time to call a friend or parent, answer emails, or listen to music or a podcast. Or maybe you prefer to zone out, observing your surroundings, thinking about upcoming tasks, or just letting your mind wander. Either way, those miles will add up, so once you finally get home for the night, you can feel good about your level of physical activity and really enjoy some relaxation before bed.

TAKE CARE OF YOUR LUNGS

It is no secret that smoking cigarettes takes a toll on your lungs and overall health. Whether you smoke every once in a while, like at a party with friends, or every single day, there is truly no safe way to smoke. Unfortunately, you can still feel pressure—whether it's from a peer or the stress of a current class project—to reach for a cigarette. You may have even started the school year already smoking, and are now struggling to stop or at least start cutting back.

If you do find yourself in one of these situations, reach out for support. Campus wellness centers will typically have everything from hotline numbers to support groups—or information about where to find a local group. And if you haven't smoked, but feel pressure to do so, there are things you can do to curb the temptation. You can chew gum, eat a healthy snack, or drink a glass of water. It can also help to think of the benefits of walking away from the habit. Not smoking lowers your risk of lung cancer and heart disease, protects those around you from secondhand smoke, makes it easier to breathe, and promotes endurance during exercise.

GO FOR A RUN ON CAMPUS

Whether you're a competitive runner, a casual weekend jogger, or a student just trying to make healthier choices 1 mile at a time, a speedy jog can provide a much-needed distraction from stress, not to mention a great workout—and your college campus is the perfect backdrop. Ask around to find out if there are any existing running clubs, or see if a friend is free to hit the pavement (or a shady path through the quad). There may even be exercise-specific tracks available, which are perfect if you're training for a race or working toward a fitness goal.

You can lace up your sneakers to stay in shape or clear your mind, for strong legs or an endorphin rush—in silence or with headphones blaring your go-to tunes. Running at your school is also a wonderful way to explore the area! You can check out the beautiful scenery, admire your campus's architecture, figure out how to navigate nearby neighborhoods—or just time the distance from your apartment building to the school bookstore so you can make it there before it closes next time.

TAKE ADVANTAGE OF WELLNESS PROGRAMS

Just like many corporate work environments nowadays, your college may have wellness incentive programs available. Be sure to take full advantage—one of the best things about being a student is the free stuff, after all! Check out your campus health center or student life organization to see what's available. Campus wellness programs can include recreational events or activities like trail rides, ski trips, or challenge courses—or access to maps and other information related to nearby outdoor activities like camping, canoeing, or fishing. In addition, check for free lectures or classes designed around wellness-related topics. These may include things like food documentaries, successful habit-building, or alcohol or drug use education. You may also be able to meet with a campus health coach or dietitian to talk about sleep, exercise, nutrition, stress or time management skills, and more; these experts can design custom plans to help you stay healthy.

STRETCH YOUR FINGERS

From essays to emails to class research, you're constantly typing on your laptop—which can lead to tension in your wrists, forearms, and fingers if left unchecked. Hand pain related to writing lecture notes for hours on end is also common. While it is often a case of writer's cramp, these issues can lead to something more serious, like carpal tunnel syndrome. It's important to regularly check in on your hands and wrists during longer periods of typing or writing. Feelings of numbness, tingling, weakness, or grip loss are all signs that your hands need a little break, and that's where some quick stretching can be most beneficial. One easy stretch exercise is to extend your hand in front of you, palm up, then use your other hand to gently pull your fingers back toward the back of your wrist. Repeat the stretch in your other hand. Do this every hour or so, particularly when you're writing long lecture notes or rushing to finish a research paper on time.

REST YOUR EYES

With your smartphone, computer, TV, and tablet, your eyes are constantly glued to a screen (it's not your fault: those chemistry reports aren't going to write themselves—though wouldn't that be great...). Between using all of these electronics, it is important to take frequent breaks to rest your eyes. This will help avoid eyestrain or dry or red eyes. You can take this break by simply closing your eyes briefly in the middle of a work session, or by using the 20-20-20 rule (look at something 20 feet away every 20 minutes for 20 seconds). Adjust the brightness on your computer as well, and use night-vision settings if possible; you can also wear blue-light-blocking glasses to help reduce eyestrain. If you do find you're spending endless hours indoors huddled in front of your laptop, head outside for a quick pause in a different visual surrounding. Final exams aren't going anywhere, but your eyesight might if you don't protect it!

PLAN YOUR WEEKLY MEALS

Some schools require that First Year students utilize a traditional meal plan at dining facilities on campus. If that's the case for you, "planning" meals may be as simple as aiming to make healthy choices—like loading up half of your plate with veggies and watching portion sizes—every time you eat a meal.

However, if you have access to a kitchen, you can plan out your specific meals every week in order to save time and money. At the beginning of every week (or on Sundays), take some time to think about your meals and snacks based on your class schedule or other commitments. You can prep meals ahead of time by cooking larger amounts of certain foods and storing them in individual serving containers, packing multiple options for long days away from your dorm, and identifying when and where you'll be eating out that week. You'll especially appreciate the effort when you wake up late one morning and have a jar of overnight oats ready to take to class.

MAKE A DOCTOR'S APPOINTMENT

Taking charge of your health begins with a simple visit to the doctor. If you're a freshman, you might have already seen your primary care provider to get certain school-mandated vaccinations before coming to campus. Still, stop by the student health center to learn about what's available. Things like regular checkups, treatment for a common cold, mental and reproductive health check-ins, dental and vision services, and access to a pharmacy should be offered at your campus health center. The center can also educate you on the nearest emergency room and urgent care facilities, as well as surrounding specialists or resources related to specific illnesses.

When you do make a doctor's appointment, make sure to check your insurance policy to figure out what is and isn't covered. And, of course, if you experience a fever, persistent symptoms, trouble breathing, odd pain or pressure, or vomiting, go to the health center. In the case of a serious injury, illness, or accident, go straight to the nearest hospital.

STAND MORE

Sitting is the new smoking, experts say, and it is no exception in school. Even if you exercise daily, you're most likely sitting down quite a bit: in your dorm room to do some reading, in the library to study for a test, in the cafeteria to eat, in a lecture hall during class. And with all of this in mind, you might wonder how you can possibly sit less—but it doesn't have to be all or nothing! Just aim to sit a little less and move a little more. For example, build a healthy habit of getting up and walking around for 5 minutes every half hour you stay seated at the library, or stand for 20 minutes after an hour-long lecture. You can also stand while you make a phone call or type an email, walk around your apartment while reading a textbook, stroll building hallways in between classes, or even see if your school has standing desks available for use. Try setting a timer on your phone as a reminder to get up and move.

BRUSH YOUR TEETH

Growing up, your parents make you brush and floss your teeth daily, but once you're at college, there's nobody to enforce dental rules, so it's easy for good habits to slip. You're also free to eat and drink whatever you want on campus, so certain unhealthy foods—like desserts and sugary drinks—can damage your teeth if you don't remember to brush or floss after eating. That doesn't mean you can't enjoy these treats in moderation, but you'll want to make adjustments to properly care for your teeth. Regularly brushing will help prevent bacteria from sticking to your tooth enamel, and brushing about 20 minutes after you have a sugary food or drink can help scrub away acid or sugar residue. Floss at least once a day, but try to do it after every meal. Swap out your toothbrush for a new one every few months, and be sure to brush your tongue too.

If you find that it's hard to remember to brush or floss, put a sticky note on your bathroom mirror, or set a reminder on your phone for the same time(s) every day. You can also keep disposable floss picks in your backpack while you're on the go.

USE YOUR CORE MUSCLES

A strong core involves much more than visible abs: it balances your center of gravity, improves your posture, and gives stability to your torso, back, pelvis, and hips. This will make it easier for you to simply get where you need to go around campus, help prevent injuries during that hike with friends, and ward off poor posture and back pain during all those hours in the library. If you play a school sport, strong core muscles also lead to better endurance, fewer muscle sprains or strains, and more energy.

To train your core, incorporate forward and side planks, bridges, and hip thrusts into your workout routine. These easy exercises can even be done in front of the TV while watching your favorite show. You can also practice using your core during daily movements, like bending down to pick up your laptop bag, leaning over to talk to a classmate, and walking to an on-campus meeting. As you move, think about tightening your midsection and drawing your belly toward your spine. No endless reps of crunches needed! Consistently engaging your core this way allows your body to avoid pain or injury related to falling down or doing physical activity.

RELAX YOUR JAW

When you're overwhelmed with homework or frustrated with a room-mate, it's natural to grit your teeth and clench your jaw as an involuntary reaction to this stress. You may be surprised at how often you're holding tension in your jaw without even realizing it! A tight jaw can lead to more serious problems over time, like headaches, chipped teeth, and tooth decay, so it's important to regularly relax your jaw.

Practice mindfully opening and closing your jaw a few times each day, letting your tongue drop off the roof of your mouth and keeping space between your lower and upper rows of teeth. You can also close your eyes and use your hands to gently massage your jaw joints (located at the base of your chin by your ears) when you feel them clenching. If you're experiencing pain or discomfort that's throbbing or tender, reach out to a dentist about getting a mouthguard or other forms of treatment to help relieve the symptoms.

ENJOY SOMETHING GREEN

A muffin and coffee at the crack of dawn, microwavable mac and cheese between study sessions, and a burger and fries for dinner? Every college student has those days where there is nary a vegetable in sight (who has the time or money to make fancy kale smoothies every day?). However, incorporating nutrient-packed veggies into your daily diet doesn't have to be complicated! Start by adding something green into every meal: put romaine on your burger, and pair your chicken and rice with steamed broccoli. Also focus on small trade-offs when possible, like choosing a lettuce wrap instead of bread for your sandwich, or chomping on kale chips instead of potato chips. These vital foods keep your skin, heart, and hair healthy, reduce your risk of cancer, and fight diabetes—so build them into your diet whenever you can!

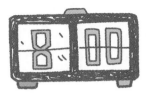

SKIP THE SNOOZE BUTTON

Sometimes you set your alarm with the best intentions, and still end up smacking the snooze button five times before finally scrambling out of the door in your pajamas—or you sleep through class entirely. Waking up early is the worst (unless you're a morning person, of course), so it's totally tempting to squeeze in as many extra minutes of sleep as possible. However, this approach essentially fools your body into reverting back to sleep mode, which can actually make you feel *more* tired throughout the day. And if you only go back to bed for a few minutes, you're unable to fall into a deep sleep anyway, missing out on the rapid eye movement (REM) sleep that restores your body.

If you struggle to get out of bed in the morning, there are a few things that can help. For one, set a real alarm clock instead of your cell phone alarm. This makes it so you're not distracted by notifications popping up (or really, anything related to your phone) first thing in the morning. This way, you can start the day more peacefully and allow for an actual morning routine, rather than falling into the social media abyss. Keep this alarm away from your bed as well, so you are forced to get up to turn it off. And if you live with someone, know each other's schedules so you have a backup buddy to wake you up if needed. Finally, when you have to get up early the next day, go to bed at a decent time to give your body the full 8 hours of rest it needs.

COUNT YOUR STEPS

Taking 10,000 steps a day has become a popular goal thanks to digital step trackers, but you don't have to walk 5 miles a day to stay healthy. Instead of trying to meet this lofty goal, focus on moving a little more throughout the day than you currently do. Use a fitness device (like a Fitbit or Apple Watch) or pedometer to track your activity. If you're unsure how to fit more steps into your daily routine, think about how you might subconsciously be taking shortcuts to classes or using the elevator to get to the fourth floor in the library. Choose the long route to your next class, and take the stairs to that study room. Park toward the back of the store parking lot when out running errands so you need to walk a little farther to get to the door. During a lecture hall break, get out of your seat and walk around instead of surfing social media. Any time you can walk, do so—and watch your steps add up!

DO A LITTLE DANCE

When you're in need of a study break, you probably reach for tried-and-true solutions, like a quick snack, a funny online video, or a walk around the block. But sometimes these tactics can get a bit stale. If you're looking to switch things up, try a dance party of one! Blast a song from your favorite album for a couple of minutes and dance your heart out to shake loose any stress and give yourself a mental break. Dancing is proven to be therapeutic, providing both a positive distraction *and* some physical movement. As a result, you'll experience a better mood, improved focus, sharpened problem-solving skills, and stronger muscles and coordination. Your dance moves don't have to be anything special, either: just move and groove to the beat as you feel your heart pumping. Bonus points if you sing along.

OPT FOR LESS SUGAR

Orange juice, vanilla lattes, energy drinks, sweet teas, lemonade—yum, right? Of course...so long as you don't have all of them, every single day! Too many drinks with added sugar or artificial sweetener can cause weight gain, increased risk of diabetes, and higher potential for heart disease over time. Unfortunately, these types of drinks are everywhere you turn—vending machines, dining hall dispensers, your dorm common room—and you're more likely to lean on them for an energy boost when the post-chem lab slump hits.

The next time you start to reach for a sugary beverage, choose still or sparkling water, or a drink sweetened with stevia, instead. Work toward making these changes whenever you can. Then, on the days when you really need a lift, you want a reward for finishing a challenging assignment, or you are simply craving the taste of a certain sweet drink, you can treat yourself without the guilt.

USE A FACE MASK

Face masks are quite the consumer favorite—and for good reason: they offer affordable options for every type of skin or skin problem. From sheets and gel masks to shower-friendly versions to clay, there is a face mask for everyone. The stress from homework, classes, and social situations, in particular, can wreak havoc on your skin, and face masks are a quick, easy way to pamper yourself and treat any pesky dark circles, oily pores, dullness, or acne. They also help prevent fine lines and aging spots. You can splurge on a fancy brand, find cheap options at the local drugstore, or try a DIY version at home (just combine ripe banana, honey, and raw oatmeal or brown sugar with a little coconut oil for an easy homemade mask). Keep a couple extra masks in your bathroom for nights when you need a little extra TLC, or for weekend spa dates with friends!

DRESS UP

Good ol' sweats. They might as well be the unofficial uniform of every college. And sure, they are supercomfy—almost like bringing a piece of your bed to class with you—but comfort doesn't always correlate to a good mood. In fact, wearing sweatpants, yoga pants, sweatshirts, or other comfortable-yet-drab clothing can affect your self-confidence. The old adage is true: when you look your best, you feel your best.

Making an effort to dress up a bit more for things like an internship or presentation, or just on a rainy Sunday when you are feeling down, is an easy way to build confidence and promote productivity. Whether it's jeans and a clean shirt, or a more stylish ensemble, choosing to dress up even when those sweats are calling your name will help you feel ready to handle anything and everything that comes your way.

SOAK UP THE SUN

For all the emphasis on sun protection (which is important), you still want to get a good dose of vitamin D every day. A by-product of the sun's rays, vitamin D is associated with an improved mood, better sleep, lower blood pressure, and stronger bones. Now, that doesn't mean you should go lie on a grassy hill with tanning oil and no sunscreen on the next time you are in the mood for an outdoor study sesh; getting just 10–20 minutes of sun exposure is enough to benefit—especially when the sun hits your shoulders, arms, and legs. If you suffer from a skin condition like eczema or psoriasis, ask your doctor if extra sunlight may also help minimize symptoms. And for those struggling with stress or seasonal depression (often known as seasonal affective disorder), sunshine can be especially helpful in easing stress and lifting your mood. Some research even indicates that sunshine can help students perform better on tests—a fantastic reason to get outside before your next exam!

CHAPTER 2
BOOST YOUR BRAIN: MENTAL SELF-CARE

Caring for your mental health isn't as straightforward as physical self-care is, but it's just as crucial. Depending on your personal needs, mental well-being may focus on keeping your brain sharp by giving it time to recharge after an intense class discussion, or playing mental games in your free time to strengthen memory recall and protect against diseases like dementia and Alzheimer's. Your mental health might require treatment for something like post-traumatic stress disorder, bipolar disorder, ADHD, clinical depression, or anxiety disorder. Mental self-care varies from person to person, and also changes from day to day, so it's always good to experiment with different activities to see what works best for you. You may also benefit from connecting with an on-campus professional for further support.

This chapter is full of easy ways to nurture your mental health, from fun games to promote creativity and boost your ability to retain information, to stimulating activities beyond your dorm room. You will explore strategies for calming a racing mind, getting control of your thoughts, and giving yourself a mental break when needed—so you can make your brain work harder *and* smarter (no cardio required!).

TRY THE 90-MINUTE SPRINT

You might be used to hiding out in your room, trying to memorize vast quantities of information for hours on end. Or maybe you often find yourself staring at a blinking cursor at 10 p.m., unsure of where to begin an essay that you've technically been *trying* to write all day. Though it may seem like working more equals getting more done, prolonged work sessions don't actually lead to more productivity—just work overload. Your brain can only focus for 90–120 minutes at a time, which is why shorter work sprints of that length can do wonders for your attention span and output.

Break your work into blocks of time (if 90 minutes seems too long, 30–60 minute stretches will also work), and then focus on doing one thing during each block. Read the next two chapters of your book, make twenty-five flash cards, write two pages of your research paper, etc. Set a timer for each block as well, and turn off all distractions: close your email, put your phone on airplane mode, quit playing a TV show in the background. Work until the 90 (or 30–60) minutes are up, take a break, and come back for the next "sprint" feeling refreshed.

SLOW YOUR SCROLL

Here's the thing about social media (and the Internet in general): it's designed to keep you scrolling so your attention is engaged for as long as possible. Content seems endless because *it is*, and every time you open up a tab to *BuzzFeed*, *College Humor*, or *theSkimm* before class starts (or during class—let's be honest) or check Snapchat and WhatsApp during a study break, more content will appear to keep you coming back for more. Addictive, right? That's why so many people get stuck in the habit of browsing and scrolling any time they have a free moment or receive a push notification (or just want to avoid falling asleep during a boring lecture).

Even just a couple hours away from social media and the web can improve your mental health. It elevates your mood, improves sleep, and helps you be more present in the moment—it's even linked to better school performance! To slow down your scroll, use the desktop versions of social media platforms. Yes, they're less user-friendly and eye-grabbing than the app versions, but they'll also help you look at content more purposefully instead of mindlessly tapping and swiping. Also be sure to log out of apps on your phone or computer after using them so you have to manually log in to read or look at something later. This "inconvenience" offers a quick checkpoint to make sure you really want to engage with digital media versus using it as a stopgap or distraction.

GET LOST IN A BOOK

In college, reading often seems to be directly connected to homework. It's no wonder students everywhere struggle with finding the motivation to crack open a book. But reading doesn't have to be boring, stressful, or otherwise unenjoyable! A good book develops your imagination, expands your perception of the world, and teaches you how to connect the dots between different ideas; you learn how to interpret, comprehend, and react to themes, characters and plotlines that can often be applied to real life. Reading for pleasure is much more than gathering information, memorizing facts, or only reading about topics you think you "should" care about.

There are also countless options beyond that history textbook you have yet to open. If you're not sure where to start, go to the library or a local bookstore and just browse: pick up whatever attracts your interest. You can also listen to an audiobook to ease back into the habit of reading, or look up books that your favorite movies and TV shows are based on. Be sure to ask for recommendations from friends and family members as well, since they know your tastes best.

TAKE A SHORT STUDY BREAK

You're never too busy to take a break. No, this doesn't give you a permission slip to watch forty *YouTube* videos in a row instead of studying, but it does mean you need to pay attention to your energy levels and take breaks accordingly. For example, if you have trouble concentrating—are fidgety and restless, or annoyed by everyone around you—that's not a green light to push through and down another espresso. It's actually a red flag that your mind needs a time-out. Your mental capacity is renewable, but you have to give yourself plenty of time to rest in order for your brain to hit that refresh button.

Build breaks into your study time. Keep the length of each break relatively short—from a minute or two, up to 10–20 minutes—and do something restorative during that break: walk around your dorm room, listen to an upbeat song, eat a nourishing snack, drink a cold glass of water, do some jumping jacks, or take a catnap. Think of study breaks as the links between long periods of productivity; you need them to perform your best.

LEARN A NEW SKILL

College is the place where you build the skills necessary to find a job— and it's beneficial no matter how many years you have left of school. For example, maybe you want to improve your communication abilities, so you take a public speaking course to practice presenting to a group, or you volunteer to answer questions in class. Pretty soon, you'll notice how those new communication skills aid in every part of your life, from academics to personal relationships.

Choose something that you would like to learn or improve on, and take the necessary steps to reach that goal. You can go to the campus writing center to refine your writing, editing, and proofreading tactics, which will enable you to express yourself clearly, catch typos and logical errors in your thinking, and put together a cover letter and resume. Or maybe you are interested in computer code, search engine optimization, a foreign language, photography, or video editing. Sign up for a class either on or off campus, check out online tutorials, or even ask a talented friend to show you the ropes.

ELIMINATE A STRESSOR

Sometimes stressors in life are completely outside of your control, but other times you may be able to eliminate the source. In order to do this, first take note of what's causing you angst or anxiety. Next, consider if it's something you can remove from your life. For example, maybe you frequently spend time with a casual acquaintance you met during orientation week, but the encounters always leave you feeling self-critical or frustrated. You can then cut down on your interactions with that person and focus on spending time with people who do make you feel good. Or maybe you wake up late and miss your first class. You can choose to let that ruin your whole attitude for the day, or you can take a deep breath and learn from the mistake by going to bed early that night and making sure your alarm is properly set for tomorrow. Whatever is within your control and causing you stress, take a step toward eliminating it.

LISTEN TO A PODCAST

Podcasts are an excellent way to learn and laugh without needing to carry around a book or stare at a screen. You can throw your headphones on while heading to the gym and listen to information on all kinds of topics such as the news, technology, pop culture, comedy, or personal development; you can multitask by listening to a podcast while driving across campus, doing the dishes, or walking to a restaurant for dinner with a friend. There are thousands of choices out there to fit your unique interests or educational goals; you can pick one based on an interest in money hacks or habit-building, or a love for stand-up comedy. There are even college-specific podcasts that you can listen to regarding the application process, financial aid, dorm room organization, late admissions, and so much more. Best of all, they are free and easy to download right to your phone!

PUT A STOP TO HARMFUL RUMINATION

Ruminating occurs when you obsess over a negative situation. Your thoughts feel like a broken record as you replay an interaction nonstop or brood over an event that happened in the past. Anything can be a trigger—that time you said something "dumb" to the barista, failed a pop quiz, or experienced a bad first date—and this mode of thinking usually makes you feel downright awful. It also distracts you from the present moment, and it is not helpful to your personal growth.

To switch gears and stop ruminating, first focus on identifying what exactly is bothering you. Then, consider the (realistic) worst-case scenario, and ask yourself, "So what?" For example, perhaps you're overanalyzing an interview and fear that you didn't make the cut. Worrying isn't going to help you get the job, and even if you don't get it, things will be okay. Yes, it will be a bummer, but there are plenty of other great opportunities out there. Laying out the facts can help you let go of what has already happened and view mistakes as chances to learn and grow.

WRITE LECTURE NOTES BY HAND

You probably write all of your class notes on a keyboard. Hey, it's fast and efficient, and it aligns with the technology that your professor is probably already using in the class. However, writing by hand helps you remember more information, organize and expand your thoughts, and increase creativity and deep thought. When using the "old-fashioned" way, your brain has to work harder to support your motor skills. The slower pace of handwriting also forces you to listen to and comprehend large amounts of information to figure out what you need to capture on paper and what you can skip (versus typing everything verbatim without processing any meaning). It also promotes a state of mental flow, due to the rhythmic quality of putting pen to paper as you digest and summarize what you hear and see. Use a notebook to jot down notes by hand at your next lecture; you'll likely walk out of class feeling more familiar with the material.

SWITCH UP YOUR STUDY SCENERY

Humans are creatures of habit: we like our routines to stay the same so that we know what to expect and can maintain a measure of control. You undoubtedly experience this on campus too. Maybe you always study in the same corner cubicle, or listen to an album on repeat to get in the zone, or rely on a matcha-tea-and-scone combination every time you're diving into notes before a test. However, experts say that occasionally switching up locations when studying can lead to improved information retention. Because your brain is more keenly aware of the new sights, smells, and sounds of your surroundings, it makes associations between the information you are processing and those sensory experiences.

If you always go to the library, try out the tutoring center today. If you primarily stay on campus, head to a local lunch spot and grab a table at which to eat while you study. Bring your textbooks and a blanket to the park if the weather is nice, or use a long commute to page through your course materials.

DRAW SOMETHING FROM MEMORY

Unless you're taking an art class, you may not spend much of your time in college drawing beyond the occasional bored doodle during a lecture. What you may not know, however, is that your brain majorly benefits from this activity. Drawing helps with visualization, improves attention to detail, enhances creativity, and develops better hand-eye coordination. Each side of your brain is called into action when you draw, and as you build new mental connections, you also practice honing your "eye" for composition, measurement, distance, and scale—relevant skills for students in any field, from video game development, to fashion design, to architecture. And when you specifically try to draw something from memory, you're translating an image in your head onto a piece of paper, which revs up your brain even more.

Start with something simple, like drawing your beloved pup from home, your old bedroom, or the outside of your favorite greasy spoon diner near campus. Don't worry too much about getting it exactly right, either. And if you want more opportunities to draw, take a basic beginners' class, or see if there's a figure-drawing course available as an elective.

CREATE A MORNING ROUTINE

You wake up 12 minutes before your first class, throwing on the nearest (clean) clothes and rushing out the door with a piece of toast in hand. Sound like a typical day? While it may seem like this is just how things are for a busy college student with classes to get to and people to meet up with, you can make things run a lot smoother by setting a morning routine. To create this routine, simply allot a set amount of time (at least 10 minutes) each morning to do whatever will help prepare you for the day ahead. You can practice yoga stretches in your bed while your coffee brews, primp in the mirror while jamming to music, or review your schedule while scrambling eggs. Maybe you use your morning routine to get stuff done, like catching up on schoolwork, or to focus on yourself by taking a long shower or meditating. When you start the day on a positive note, you set the tone for the rest of the day.

50..49..48

COUNT BACKWARD FROM FIFTY

You obviously know how to count—but counting backward pushes your brain just a little further by forcing it to do something it's not as used to doing. This exercise redirects your attention from any negative thoughts or worries to the present moment. As a student, you can use this simple activity anytime you feel overwhelmed or unfocused—which may be pretty often! You can start with the number fifty, then go higher or lower depending on what is best for you. When you count, you can do so aloud or in your head. It's kind of like a simple mini-meditation you can do anywhere, including at home before bed if you're having trouble sleeping. Also feel free to experiment with different variations on this exercise, like counting down by fours or other multiples, going faster or slower, or even alternating between numbers and letters of the alphabet.

DO A JIGSAW PUZZLE

Puzzles aren't just for retirement homes and senior citizens. In fact, working on a puzzle is a great de-stressing activity to do either by yourself after an intense biology lab, or with a group of friends to mentally reset at the end of a school week. Difficulty levels range, too, so you can pick an easy jigsaw when you want to chill out but also keep your hands and mind busy, or a more complicated one thousand–piece set if you're in the mood for a challenge. Chill or challenge, puzzles boost your critical-thinking skills, stimulate your brain, build confidence, and teach you to think outside the box.

And the more you practice spotting visual connections, recognizing patterns, and following your intuition, the more you can put these skills to the test when solving problems in the real world. For example, let's say you're creating a big presentation for your boss somewhere down the road. These skills can help you think through all the needed visuals, along with what copy or scripting needs to be done, and whether there is any duplicative information that needs to be removed.

SING A FAVORITE SONG

If you need a quick mood-lift between homework assignments or classes, singing can do the trick! Belting out your favorite tune releases feel-good endorphins in your brain, improves mental function and memory, supports immunity, and gives your lungs a solid workout. You can sing in the dorm shower, your car, or a karaoke bar with friends. You can even join a college choir or choral ensemble to work singing into your regular routine. Beyond boosting your mood, singing in a group is a great way to widen your social circle and be part of your college community. If you decide that singing is a true passion for you, you can also check out a local professional choir or start a cover band on campus. So anytime you feel stress creeping in, sing along to one of your favorites to get back on track!

BREAK UP A BIG TASK

Let's say you have a movie review due for film class tomorrow and you haven't started. Feeling overwhelmed, you start to panic, thinking, "How am I ever going to get this done?" Not knowing where to start, you might spiral deeper into procrastination. Hold on a minute! There's a simple solution: take that larger assignment and break it into smaller tasks. Start by writing down everything you need to do for the review: watch the movie, take notes, look up details wherever you need more information, review the notes for larger themes and other relevant insights, create an outline of your opinions, write a review introduction, write a first draft, write a conclusion, edit the full review, and so on. By identifying all of the smaller things you need to do, completing the review (or take-home exam or lab report) feels more manageable, you have a plan of action, *and* you avoid going into panic mode.

WATCH A FUNNY VIDEO

If you've ever clicked on a video of a dancing dog to get your mind off of something negative, you already know how laughter can affect your mental health. Humor lifts your mood, promotes a positive mind-set, and reduces anxiety and depression. It also calms stress hormones in your body. When you're in a calmer state, your blood pressure decreases, and the physical act of laughing sends dopamine to your brain as a reward, encouraging your immune system to work better and increasing your brain's ability to remember and recall information. Sure, you want to avoid going down the rabbit hole, watching hours of videos to distract yourself from pressing obligations. However, taking some time to look at something that makes you laugh is an easy way to regroup after taking a tough exam or seeing your student loan balance. Stream a stand-up comedy special, watch pranks, put on an episode of a funny show, or post a meme—whatever has you laughing out loud.

PLAY A MUSICAL INSTRUMENT

Haven't picked up a keyboard since high school? Not sure what a treble clef even is? College is the perfect place to learn (or relearn) how to play a musical instrument. From classes and private lessons to open music halls, there are tons of opportunities to try an instrument you are curious about or to sharpen up rusty skills.

Just listening to music activates almost every part of your brain—from your cerebellum (which controls your senses and motor movements), to your hippocampus and frontal lobes (which tap your memory and language centers)—and connects the dots between different cognitive functions. And then there's the act of playing that music yourself. From reading sheet music to translating those notes to the different keys, there's so much going on when you play an instrument. Staying focused, processing what you are reading, and creating sounds that won't send your roommates fleeing to the library all challenge your brain, strengthening its abilities to retain and process information and increasing your resilience to age-related health issues. It is also shown to help you make better choices and even regulate your mood! Playing music can be an extracurricular activity between classes and homework, or even a fun class you earn credits for.

ASK A QUESTION

Everyone has felt the fear of asking a silly question in front of a packed lecture hall; raising your hand takes courage. It is also an easy way to care for your mental health! When you ask a question and receive the answer, the exchange forms new patterns in your brain that promote mental flexibility and creates more space for new ideas. This in turn can lead to better perception of different perspectives. It also helps you fully understand and remember information, which is useful not only for studying, but also for carrying information over to the working world. That classic "there are no stupid questions" sentiment? Especially true as a college student—in college, the entire point is for you to learn as much as possible! So ask questions—of your peers, your parents, your professors—and don't be shy about what you don't know. Sometimes it just takes practice to get over nerves or uncertainty, so do a trial run with a friend, ask a stranger for directions one day (and then the next for more practice!), or sign up for a class that involves interview skills.

GET INTO A STATE OF FLOW

"Flow" is a term you may have heard floating around in conversations with peers or on social media, but may not know the full meaning of. In short, "flow" describes the mental state of being completely absorbed by an activity. You're focused and present, harnessing your energy for a particular task (and not realizing that 2 hours have slipped away since you looked at the clock). A state of flow can happen with all types of activities, like writing a paper on a topic you feel passionate about, or playing Ultimate Frisbee with your friends. You can consciously place yourself in a state of flow, too, whenever you're engaging in something that is challenging, like learning a new educational concept or taking part in a campus-wide race. The more you access your flow, the more productive you can be. You will get that history report done much faster than if you struggled through it feeling unfocused.

To usher in a state of flow, minimize distractions. For example, if you're trying to focus your attention on homework, wear headphones, set a timer, and turn off other electronics. It may also help to sit in an area without a window or other people around to attract your attention.

PLAY SUDOKU

Sudoku is a simple way to give your brain some additional exercise. Each puzzle has boxes with empty spaces and some numbers already inserted. You then have to fill in the blank spots. Sounds a little too easy at first—but it is actually quite the fun challenge! Sudoku pushes your mind to solve problems creatively, make quick decisions, and note patterns, relationships, and strategies in order to figure out which numbers should go where. This impacts your logical and critical-thinking skills, so you're better able to analyze and process information in those lengthy lectures, as well as minimize your risk of being manipulated by peers who may not have your best interests at heart.

If numbers aren't your thing, you can try any type of memory training game related to sequences or combinations, like crossword puzzles, word searches, or chess. Play online for free, buy a book of puzzles, or download printable versions (perfect for the next time you're flying home to see family). You can also see if there are groups or tournaments available for these kinds of games at your school; you can meet peers who share your interest, and take a much-needed break from studying for that exam.

TAKE A VITAMIN

Ideally, a well-balanced diet gives you all the vitamins you need to keep your brain strong and vibrant. In reality, however, college life means you may not always fit everything into your daily meals. Classes, homework, and social obligations can mean you live on nachos and pancakes one day and ramen noodles the next. Even if you are mindful about eating healthy in college, nutritional supplements like multivitamins and probiotics are an easy way to add more nutrients to your diet. Vitamin B_{12} and omega-3 fatty acids (also known as fish oil) can help prevent memory loss, while vitamin D promotes strong bones and teeth, and vitamin C helps protect against sickness. You should talk to your doctor about which vitamins would be most helpful for you depending on your current health. There are even gummy versions to make vitamins go down a bit easier!

BE VULNERABLE

College is an amazing opportunity for new experiences and the freedom to explore your passions—and it's also a time of vulnerability. You're trying to figure out just who you are and what you want out of life, and that can be scary. But being vulnerable doesn't have to be a bad thing; in fact, it is actually a great way to work in a little self-care! Being vulnerable allows you to establish and strengthen relationships with others so you have more support when you do go outside your comfort zone for a new experience—or realize something you thought you loved isn't really for you. Being vulnerable also helps you grow as an individual, as you learn how to handle both the risks and the rewards of opening yourself up in this way.

To practice, pay attention to any topics or situations that bring up a "fight-or-flight" instinct. Instead of following that instinct, take a deep breath and reflect on your needs, thoughts, and emotions in the moment. If you're bummed by a bad grade on a test and your roommate asks how your day went, allow yourself to share feelings of disappointment instead of insisting on being "fine." And when someone offers to support you as a result—like if that same roommate tries to cheer you up with a hug or funny joke—let them, instead of putting up a wall.

MAKE SOMETHING WITH YOUR HANDS

Working with your hands isn't just for engineering majors! Research has proven that activities where you're making something tangible (like a sculpture or piece of furniture) can decrease stress and anxiety and lead to better overall mental health. This is because the process of using your hands in an intentional way to repair or create feels satisfying and promotes creativity and problem-solving. You might already be familiar with this sensation, like when you had to put together that tricky bookshelf for your dorm room! This practice is a great way to distract your mind when you feel that pre-exam anxiety creeping in, or relieve stress after a challenging class.

Most schools have all kinds of options for working with your hands, from a robotics or construction materials course to a peer group focused on learning how to make Italian food. You can also check out social media accounts to find videos and tutorials on tons of different crafts.

LEARN YOUR BURNOUT SIGNALS

With demanding schedules, sleepless nights, hard assignments, and new relationships, stress in college can slowly creep from manageable to crushing. That's when burnout hits. More than just a bad day, burnout is when you're mentally and physically depleted; you're feeling down, frustrated, and exhausted, and you can't really put your finger on one specific reason why (which is even more frustrating!). Other signs can include a lack of motivation or concentration, an inability to remember information, low energy or fatigue, and difficulty staying interested in anything. You might wonder if burnout is just a reality—after all, your roommates may be experiencing it, too, and isn't college *supposed* to be stressful? It often can be, sure, but burnout is not the norm.

When you notice yourself feeling the symptoms of burnout, it's time to slow down and practice some extra self-care. Disconnect from technology if you can, reconnect with friends or family members, and add more breaks into your daily routine. You may also benefit from talking to a campus therapist or your student affairs department for more guidance.

DAYDREAM FOR 15 MINUTES

You have probably been told for years that daydreaming is a negative distraction. No more! Daydreaming actually activates your working memory, which allows your brain to consider several thoughts at once. With your working memory activated, you're better equipped for complex problem-solving, productivity, and creativity. Without a strong working memory, your brain would space out entirely, like when you're reading a chapter in your textbook and realize you didn't actually grasp anything in it. When you daydream for short periods of time, your mind also has room to contemplate current situations or problems. For example, a brilliant thesis idea may pop into your head while you're in the shower, even though you couldn't come up with anything when you were sitting at your desk all day. So, when you feel stuck on an assignment or unable to focus on an essay, let your mind wander for 10–15 minutes. You'll come back to the task at hand feeling refreshed and ready to get things done.

GO SOMEWHERE NEW

New experiences in general are terrific for your brain, and college is full of opportunities to explore. You don't have to break the bank or even leave campus, either: maybe you switch up your Saturday night plans by hitting up a concert in the auditorium instead of the usual house party, or maybe you check out the sports stadium one afternoon versus lingering in the library. Of course, you can also do something more involved, like applying for a study abroad program or traveling out of state during your fall break.

Anytime you go someplace new, you encounter uncertainty, which builds more neural pathways in your mind and helps develop mental fortitude. Faced with change, you are also encouraged to practice empathy and creativity. Plus, you get to cultivate new stories and friendships along the way!

SQUEEZE A STRESS BALL

If you're stressing over an upcoming exam or whether to change your major, squeezing a stress ball is an easy way to take the edge off. These low-cost foam, sand, or gel-filled balls come in tons of different shapes and sizes—you may have even received one in your orientation package or at a campus event. While it sounds simple (a little too simple to be true, even), the act of repetitively gripping and releasing a stress ball relieves stress and promotes overall relaxation. How? Stress causes a fight-or-flight reaction in your body, but when you're sitting in your dorm room waiting for a deadline to approach, all that negative energy has nowhere to go. A stress ball is the perfect tool for redirecting that energy—plus, it is fun. You can carry your stress ball in your book bag or purse and pull it out anytime you need a distraction from the daily grind of assignments and exams.

START A JOURNAL

Maybe you kept a diary as a kid, or you scrawled down your thoughts in a notebook as part of a class project in middle or high school. Well, it's time to pick up that pencil (or pen) again! Journaling is an easy way to get your creative juices flowing and your mental gears turning—plus, it's great practice for all of those essays you have to write. The physical act of writing taps into your analytical left brain, while the thought needed to come up with what to actually write opens up your creative, emotional right brain. When both parts are working together, you get the best of both worlds. For example, writing down the events of your day helps you when it comes time to write that long biology report next week. Venturing into your thoughts and feelings in your journal opens the door to new ideas and solutions to any problems you may have been stuck on in either your homework or a personal situation.

Journaling doesn't need to take up a ton of time, either: just 15–20 minutes a day can increase your vocabulary, memory, and comprehension skills; bring clarity to any confusing thoughts; and help you feel relaxed and focused. Tailor your journal to what you need: inspirational quotes and writing prompts, bullet points to keep track of homework or plan out social events, things you're proud of, situations you're struggling with, or goals you want to work on.

CREATE A CUSTOM PLAYLIST

There's something so satisfying about making the perfect playlist for an occasion—and science backs up the good vibes. Music triggers a dopamine rush in your brain, and research shows that this increase can lower blood pressure, reduce anxiety, and improve your mood. Think of how high-tempo, upbeat songs give you the motivation and energy to run faster on the indoor track at your athletic center—or how unexpectedly hearing a classic oldies song in the dining hall makes you smile. Now put that to good use! Create custom playlists for specific activities, like getting ready in the morning before class, studying late at night, moving into your own place off campus, or celebrating the first Friday night of a new semester. Then, just hit "play"!

VISIT A MUSEUM

Most of the time, you're focused on getting things done: finishing that last economics assignment, watching those Spanish video tutorials, taking your religious studies midterm. It's a lot! And eventually, you may hit a mental wall where it feels like you can't possibly cram one more piece of information into your brain. This is when getting off campus can be a key to your self-care. Away from your busy routine, you can hit the "refresh" button and shed any negative energy that may have been weighing you down.

A trip to a museum is the perfect destination for your adventure off campus! No matter the type of museum you choose—art, natural history, aviation, technology—you're surrounded by artifacts and information that will broaden your intellect and also allow you to recharge your mind. Take a self-guided tour of a gallery, or check out campus bulletin boards for group trips to local museums. And don't forget to ask about student discounts! Most museums offer a free pass (or at least lower admission rates) for students.

CLEAN OUT YOUR BAG

When you're constantly traveling from class to class, your book bag or purse holds a lot of stuff: tissues, ChapStick, an extra hoodie, your wallet and student identification card, a phone, flash drives, snacks, gum, a water bottle, miscellaneous pens and highlighters—and probably a lot more. All that clutter weighs you down both physically (your shoulders and back might even be hurting lately from lugging around a heavy bag every day!) *and* mentally. It's true: studies have found that physical clutter overloads your senses and serves as a distraction, leading to stress, foggy thinking, and poor performance. Whether you're throwing things in your bag "just in case" or you're truly in need of each item on a day-to-day basis, every once in a while, clean out what you carry to start fresh. Get tidy so you can truly focus on that philosophy paper.

OPEN THE WINDOWS

Whether it's in classrooms, the library, or a work-study program, you are cooped up all day—which is exactly why opening a window is the (literal) breath of fresh air you need! Depending on the weather, you might be able to take your studies outside or go for a long walk before you focus on a demanding research paper. But if that's not an option, the mere act of exposing your lungs to clean air by cracking a window will work wonders on your mental health. Oxygen promotes the release of serotonin in your body, which sends more power to your brain, makes you feel happier, and gives your body some natural energy. Serotonin also helps you naturally wake up (no matter the time of day) and relaxes your nervous system. So open that window and take a deep breath—bonus points if you spend a little extra time soaking in the sights, sounds, and smells of nature (it helps improve short-term memory and concentration!).

LEAVE YOUR PHONE AT HOME

Is your smartphone glued to your hip 24/7? If the answer is yes (which, let's face it—just about everyone's answer is), it's time to live without it—for a short time, anyway. Phones (and other electronic devices) may allow you to stay connected to friends and family back home, but it's easy to become crazy reliant on them, too, which does a number on your mental health. After all, looking at your phone constantly can really mess with your ability to concentrate in class. Too much phone use can also impact relationships, like when your roommate or partner keeps checking social media when you're trying to spend quality time with them.

Research recommends leaving your phone behind when stepping out, like for the walk to grab lunch or when catching up with friends in person around campus. When you do, notice any bad habits that crop up as a result, such as feeling the need to document every single moment for others, feeling afraid of missing out, or reaching for your phone to distract yourself when bored or lonely. To break these habits, focus on tuning into the present moment: watch the facial expressions of your friend across the table, or feel the wind on your face as you stroll to the dining hall. Even allow yourself to be a little bored (hey, boredom is a great motivator for ambition and imagination!). Remember that you control your device; it doesn't control you.

HOLD A 1-MINUTE PLANK

Planks might be a part of your physical workout, but they're also a great way to build mental toughness too. Did you ever wonder why personal trainers and celebrity athletes often talk about how your mind gives up before your body? That's because it's true! A strong mind really does equal a strong body, and positions like the plank force you to face both physical and mental discomfort and push past it. When you practice holding a plank, you practice mental endurance: you overcome self-critical thoughts, encourage yourself, and commit to seeing it through to the end.

These same qualities can be applied to any difficulty you may face during your college career, from finishing a complicated assignment to learning a new trade to getting over a toxic relationship. Planks are a simple way of mentally conditioning yourself—and working on those abs. Anytime you need an extra dose of empowerment, set a timer for a 1-minute plank. Research the many variations of plank poses: for example, to the side or straight across; on your forearms and feet; or on your hands and knees.

FLIP THROUGH A COMIC

Yes, comics, cartoons, and graphic novels all count as reading—and they're an easy way to stretch your mental muscles. For one thing, the more you read (regardless of the material), the smarter you become. Better yet, research indicates that comics in particular actually change the neuron activity in your brain, promoting deep reading. In simpler terms, you have to focus on the layout of each page while reading the dialogue and also paying attention to important visuals. Making meaning out of visual, spatial, and textual elements is a complex activity for your brain—and much more than just "looking at pictures." The improved comprehension and analytical skills that come from reading comics are also beneficial to your brain's ability to make connections, increase vocabulary, and process nuanced themes. In other words, reading comics can actually make you smarter—and make understanding those long, complicated texts in your classes a breeze (well, a bit easier, at least).

Not sure what comics you should read? Start by asking a student library assistant for recommendations or checking out any manga or comic book clubs on campus. Your school may also offer workshops that teach you how to write and design your own comics!

SNACK ON FRUIT

Good nutrition is linked to good mental health. Research shows that snacking on fruit (the whole and natural kind—like an apple instead of applesauce!) improves your mood and reduces symptoms of depression and anxiety, which will help you better cope with stress and perform well in your classes. Of course, eating healthy is hard when you're already stressed or trying to get to a lecture on time, making it easy to fall into bad habits on the go. Rather than trying to aim for a perfect diet, you can reach for healthy fruits during those late-night study sessions, or as a portable breakfast on your morning walk to class. Full of natural sugar, fruit also won't send you crashing later on like foods with artificial sugars do, which makes it a better choice than a cookie when you're trying to power through homework.

If you need a mental boost, eat berries, citrus, or pomegranates, which are full of antioxidants and can help with cancer prevention. Apples reduce inflammation and are full of fiber, which allows you stay full longer (perfect for holding off hunger between an after-class meeting and dinnertime). Low-sugar dried fruits, like cranberries, cherries, and raisins, are great for staying focused while studying. And since tomatoes are technically a fruit as well, enjoy them in salads, pasta, or sandwiches, as they can help stabilize your mood!

CHAPTER 3
NOURISH YOUR SPIRIT: SPIRITUAL SELF-CARE

What better place to explore the complex world of spirituality than college? No, really—think about it: you are surrounded by so many diverse groups and individuals, inspiring and informative classes, and unexpected learning experiences every day! With all of this at your disposal, you can figure out what you believe, explore different faith traditions, or grow in your own unique set of beliefs. And spiritual self-care is here to help. Spiritual self-care acts as a guide on this personal journey, helping you to stay curious and continue learning and developing your beliefs. Spiritual healing isn't just about faith, either: practicing spiritual self-care can also mean exploring or reconnecting with personal values, finding purpose in your own life, or even using mindfulness to be completely in the present moment, tap into the universe around you, and more.

This chapter offers a wide range of activities to help you explore and expand your spirituality, and nourish your spirit—from gratitude lists to essential oils to volunteer work. You'll discover strategies for finding meaning in your own life, and bringing meaning into the lives of others too. From prayer to acupuncture to meditation, let this chapter be your personal guru!

ATTEND A WORSHIP SERVICE

Whether you go to your place of worship every week, once in a while for major holidays, or, um, never, college gives you the space and opportunity to consider which path feels right for you, pursue any questions you may have, and form deep connections with your peers.

Most campuses (regardless of religious affiliation) have full weekend services and weeknight worship, prayer services, and daily devotion time. Each event is a little different, and may include music, silence, reflection, and/or liturgical texts. You'll probably be able to choose from various service lengths, too, like an "open house" style (where you can stop by a campus place of worship anytime you want to for as long as you want) or a 60–90-minute formal service. It's worth checking out all kinds of services to see which ones feel like a good fit. And if you're short on time due to homework, or don't have a ride to get to a worship location, you can even try out an online worship service!

CONTRIBUTE TO A CAUSE

Most of your dollars are probably going toward takeout, textbooks, and gas, but all you need is spare change to make an impactful donation. Helping others feels great, and when you give to a cause or organization that affirms your values, it gives you purpose and ramps up those feel-good vibes even more. Luckily, there are tons of student groups on campus to help you figure out what matters to you and where you believe your money can make a difference. Maybe you're passionate about animal rights, environmental conservation, international disaster relief, or public health. Or maybe you want to raise money to support research related to your major, like fundraising for a dance marathon event to help cure cancer, if you're pre-med. You can start a change jar to save up those quarters and collect change from roommates who want in on the effort—or give that $5 bill you probably would have blown on a second iced coffee. When you give back, you invest in what really matters.

LISTEN TO SOOTHING MUSIC

Music is a great medium for connecting to your spirituality. Both instrumental music and hymns are specifically tied to different religions, but there's a vast range of styles, genres, and songs to explore. Maybe you find that you like old-school traditional hymns—passed down through generations in your faith tradition and sung by a choir—because they make you feel like a part of something bigger than yourself. Or, you might feel drawn to more contemporary music, like blues and gospel, or praise and worship songs, that have more modern lyrics and a fresh sound. Or, instrumental tunes or melodic prayers might calm your busy mind. No matter what type of music you choose, listening to music can be inspiring, healing, and uplifting. So the next time you're feeling a general malaise of "what's the point of everything?" or just a little disconnected from your spirit, listen to some soothing music!

READ A SPIRITUAL PASSAGE

You might be thinking, "I've got way too much to read already—why would I want to add more?" Fair, but hold on a second before flipping the page! You don't need to sit down for an hour with pages and pages of text to benefit from this activity. In fact, there are tons of passages online that are short and easy to digest. And they are a great way to clear your head before jumping into the chaos of classes and social obligations, or to unwind for a few minutes before bed. Reading a spiritual text brings your mind back to a place of focus (which is especially great when you're distracted by everything you have to do before biology class at 3 p.m.). It can also provide inspiration when you're dealing with a difficult situation like an argument with your roommate.

PLAN FOR UNSTRUCTURED TIME

When you have a pocket of free time in your busy life as a college student, you probably fill it up right away with all the things you think you "should" be doing. Or, you default to activities that feel good in the moment, like endless internet videos or episodes of your favorite show, but then stress about wasting that opportunity to play catch-up. Another option? Give yourself unstructured time each day—time to do nothing. Consider it old-school playing or relaxing, where you simply do whatever you want for a half hour: nap, draw on a piece of paper, read part of a magazine, clean out your bedroom dresser drawer. You don't have to be productive, but if you're in one of those moods to tackle a random chore, go for it. Having unstructured time is like a breath of fresh air. You can view this break as a chance to reflect and practice mindfulness, or connect to a higher power by way of letting your mind wander.

VOLUNTEER IN YOUR COMMUNITY

It's hard not to feel good while, well, *doing* good. And it can give you a sense of purpose, pride, and identity, on top of more perspective on your own life (if you volunteer at a homeless shelter, it's pretty easy to count your blessings about residential housing—even when roommates are driving you crazy). You feel helpful and fulfilled, and form connections with those you're serving or helping—which reinforces those good feelings. For example, maybe you love animals. You might then find value in volunteering for a shelter or humane society. Not only are you snuggling some furry friends, but you're also caring for them and helping find them good homes.

Check out different opportunities for a cause that really speaks to you. Not sure where to start? Ask your school's career center about campus blood drives, or tutoring or coaching opportunities. And if you're part of Greek life, talk to your sorority or fraternity about participating in a volunteer activity as a group. Nonprofit organizations always need volunteers, so take a look at local bulletins as well. Not only will you make a difference for others, but you'll also learn how to be a team player, collaborate with different types of people, practice leadership skills, and get creative on behalf of a good cause.

MEDITATE

You sit down to study and are immediately bombarded with distractions: your roommate is talking on the phone, your email inbox keeps pinging as new messages come in, and last night's episode of your favorite show is calling your name. It's hard to fully concentrate on one thing when there is so much to do and think about. And that's where meditation comes in. Meditation is accessible to everyone, completely free, *and* customizable. You can meditate while walking across campus, sitting on a pillow in your dorm room, or standing in a crowded coffee shop, or before and after you hit the gym. Meditation involves focusing on your breath and tuning into yourself in order to quiet jumbled thoughts, increase your awareness for the present moment, and take time for your spiritual well-being. It's a combination of self-reflection *and* connecting to something bigger than your individual self. It helps you practice integrity and authenticity, and over time, that practice can impact how you look at yourself, the world, and your ability to serve and care for others.

You can use apps for guided meditations, listen to meditative music to get in the mood, or simply close your eyes and breathe deeply for a few minutes. Also see if your college has a meditation room or specific programs available, like student meditation retreats.

GO ON A CAMPUS MINISTRY RETREAT

Most colleges provide ministry services, which include fellowship events like volunteer, mission, or faith-based retreats. These are a great way to give back to your community, meet like-minded people, or rest and reconnect to your authentic self. Maybe you want to dive deeper into your faith tradition, or get extra guidance in your transition into college or a new major. Maybe you've been itching for the chance to ask questions about or have thoughtful discussions on topics like purpose, faith, meaning, and spirituality. Or you might just want to try something new. Whatever the reason, a campus ministry retreat may be the perfect choice for you. Retreats are open to people of all faiths (though many are rooted in specific religions) and often happen during winter, spring, or summer school breaks, so you won't have to worry about getting behind on your schoolwork if you want to participate.

MAKE A GRATITUDE LIST

Writing down what you're grateful for leads to better overall health and happiness (studies prove it!). And it can also help you pay more attention to all the things you'd otherwise take for granted. Maybe you're grateful for your parents, for helping to pay your way through college or always encouraging you to do your best. Or maybe you're grateful for the little things, like free laundry in your dorm building, a new candle that makes your room smell like home, friends who make you laugh, or canceled classes on a snowy day. Even thinking of just one thing every day can go a long way to changing your perspective for the better. And the act of writing it down makes you more aware of its impact on your life. Gratitude is like a remedy for any suffering you might experience. Take a minute to jot down anything that makes you feel thankful whenever you need a little spiritual adjustment.

PRAY

Prayer—to a deity, a loved one, or even yourself—can be a powerful form of connection. For some, it represents a more personal conversation with a higher power, where you offer thanks, ask for what you need, recite teachings, or seek guidance. You might pray for a friend about to face the toughest class in their program of study—or a parent going through a tough time now that you've left the nest—with the intent of sending your loving thoughts and words out into the universe. Or, you may use prayer to refocus yourself spiritually in a more casual way, like closing your eyes for a minute between classes to count your blessings when you feel stressed about exams or angry about a roommate situation—or to set an intention, like making more time for a significant other. Prayer can be completely customized to your values, religion, and lifestyle as a whole; it can last just 5 seconds or an hour or more, depending on what you are using it for.

BALANCE YOUR CHAKRAS

Known as the seven "energy centers" of your body, chakras can be a great indication of where your daily routine is in need of some tweaking. When exam stress, roommate troubles, shifting beliefs, and more get in the way of your personal health, your chakras will reflect that imbalance—and vice versa. For example, the solar plexus (a.k.a. the "personal power" chakra), which is connected to self-esteem, can become blocked when you start doubting yourself or your abilities following, say, a tough assignment or bad breakup. When this chakra is blocked, your confidence is on shaky ground. Larger blockages can lead to bigger issues with your self-esteem.

To find out how open or closed your own chakras may be, and how to restore balance between them, you can explore tons of online resources, like easy quizzes (e.g., the Chakra Test at EclecticEnergies.com or Chakras.info) and helpful websites (e.g., ChakraHealingSounds.com and mindbodygreen.com) that cover all the signs and healing techniques for blocked chakras.

LEARN ABOUT A DIFFERENT FAITH

Studying religion isn't just for people who want to be religious figures like priests. The more you learn about different faith traditions, the more open you become to many points of view. You also gain a deeper understanding of what other people believe, and why. And when you're trying to figure out what exactly *you* believe as a budding adult, this is especially helpful. Hey, adulting is hard enough—so why not make it even a little bit easier?

Learning about different religions also teaches you to ask more questions about topics like purpose and meaning, and life and death; you'll also build a deeper appreciation for your own faith or unique beliefs as you do figure out what they are and start to actively nurture them. Some colleges require you to take a religious studies course, but if not, it's worth considering a class.

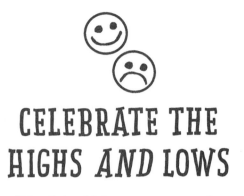

CELEBRATE THE HIGHS *AND* LOWS

Some weeks, you'll be flying high: you ace a tough exam, enjoy diner pancakes at 10 p.m. with your best friends, and wear pajamas to class every day (and don't feel guilty about it!). Other weeks, things may not go your way: you trip and fall down in front of your crush, forget to read a chapter before a pop quiz, or lose your phone during a party on the quad. Either way, it's important to both celebrate the wins of a good day or week, and acknowledge the difficulties of other times.

Being mindful of the silver lining builds resilience and helps you see the bigger picture—so you can savor everything good about your life, and then use those skills when times get tough. After all, during these crazy years (and as a graduate, too), you'll experience at least a few difficult situations, changes, and maybe even a loss of some kind (not even that "perfect" classmate in chem lab can escape this!). A strong spiritual core of appreciation for both the good *and* bad will help you bounce back stronger than ever from those inevitable lows.

SMELL AN ESSENTIAL OIL

Incense, oils, and aromas have a long history with religion and sacred ceremonies and rituals. For centuries they have been used to inspire, connect to something bigger than ourselves, and protect and purify the body, mind, and spirit. Essential oils are easy to use, and you won't have to worry about making a mess (or burning the dorm down). Cedarwood oil is perfect for spiritual grounding and purification during a meditation or prayer. It kicks to the curb negative blocks brought on by a crazy class schedule or roommate troubles—and makes your room smell great. And if you are looking for enlightenment, try rosemary oil. It stimulates deeper thought and promotes psychic development. When you are rethinking a major or trying to figure out your beliefs, rosemary oil can push you in the right direction.

Look for pure, high-quality oils that aren't diluted with chemicals or filler materials. You can use a diffuser, or apply a few drops to your wrists, your temples, the crown of your head, or behind your ears. Be sure to read the instructions and warnings on the labels carefully before putting any type of essential oil on your skin: some aren't safe for topical use, or need to be diluted in a carrier oil first. And always use with caution if you have sensitive skin.

CARVE OUT A QUIET MOMENT

Pause for a moment and pay attention to the sounds around you—a TV blaring in the background, students whispering while the professor talks, construction on campus, a dishwasher running, music playing down the hall. Most of the time, you're surrounded by all kinds of noise. It gets to be too much sometimes—and that's why taking a moment alone for real quiet is great for the soul. It creates an opportunity for spiritual reflection and encourages you to be in the present moment. And when you turn down all the noise in your life, it's easier to concentrate on connecting with your own spirit, and the universe around you. So, find somewhere quiet where you can be alone. Give yourself a little moment of silence and really tune in.

READ YOUR TAROT CARDS

If you're unfamiliar with tarot, it's a powerful and unique tool for spiritual guidance (and no, it's not just about predicting the future: there are no crystal balls required here!). Each deck has a set number of cards with images on them, each representing different spiritual lessons and personality traits. You can draw a card to meditate on or think about in relation to a current situation; you decide what the card means to you and what you do with this knowledge. For example, if you're unsure about whether to change your major to biology, you can pull a card to help you reflect on your worries and the next step to take. If you pull the Fool card, for instance, it represents new beginnings and potential. You can interpret this reading as a sign that you are ready to take the leap into that new major—and that you should feel confident doing so. The Fool is full of great opportunities, so seize the one that is right in front of you!

Tarot is meant to be an enjoyable, helpful source of wisdom—not an end-all, be-all spiritual solution. So have fun with it! Buy or borrow a deck and pull cards for yourself, or ask your friend to do it for you.

LET GO OF WHAT YOU CAN'T CONTROL

Fate. A higher power. Chance. Whatever you believe in, you know that there are always going to be things that are out of your control. Sure, it's a little scary or at least uncomfortable to think about—but it's also liberating. When you let go of what you can't control, you experience more freedom: you have the space for the thoughts, lessons, and emotions that actually serve you. And college is the perfect opportunity for learning how to let go of those things you can't control. After all, they are constantly thrown your way. For example, let's say you study really hard for an exam; you do everything possible to memorize information and prep accordingly. That part *is* in your control. After the test is over, however, you start stressing about your grade. And unfortunately, it won't be posted for another day. In the meantime, you are feeling anxious about what you got, and comparing how quickly you and the class know-it-all finished the test. So, here's the thing: worrying about it won't change anything. No matter how much you analyze the test questions after the fact, you will still get the same grade. So you might as well let go of that false sense of control, right?

Easier said than done, of course, but there are a few tips for getting started. First, make the conscious choice to let go of that worry. You can even recite something like, "I am letting go of this worry because it is unhelpful," in your head as you do. Then, get the stress out of your system; do something fun to release that negative energy and distract yourself. Finally, forgive yourself for not being perfect (nobody is!) if you don't do well on the exam, and focus on what you *can* control: how you study next time. Maybe you request a tutor, talk to your professor, or just spend more time preparing.

ASK YOUR FRIENDS ABOUT THEIR BELIEFS

Spirituality is a very personal topic for many. There are a lot of diverse beliefs and customs that come along with it—and it can feel taboo to talk about. But it's actually really important that you do. Having open, respectful discussions about beliefs helps you understand other religious views (and even better understand your own). Plus, it makes you realize just how many belief systems there are out there.

But why does it matter in college specifically? Well, because now is the time when you are really discovering and growing what exactly you believe, and why. Not to mention you are surrounded by friends and peers of so many traditions and cultural backgrounds—so take advantage! To start, try asking questions like, "Were you raised in a faith tradition?", "Do you still subscribe to the same one?", and "How has your faith changed since coming to college, if at all?" Try to stay curious, open-minded, and respectful, and ask for the same in return. The goal is not to be "right," but to better understand the people in your life.

FOCUS ON THE PRESENT

"What classes are you taking in the spring?" "Are you and your girlfriend moving in together off campus next semester?" "What field are you going to go into after graduation?" Everywhere you go people are asking about the future—and you are too. Hey, it's not a bad thing: exploring options ahead of time and making plans is all part of being prepared. Still, it can be easy to become so focused on the future that you forget to enjoy the present. Maybe you're at a party with friends, but all you can think is, "Man, I have so much homework to do before Monday." Or you have a rare snow day off from classes, and you find yourself worrying about whether you'll be able to find an internship next semester. It's time to hit the pause button. You are thinking about homework and internships when you should be living it up! Bring yourself back into the present by taking a deep breath (or five), telling your thoughts to be quiet, and observing your surroundings. This simple act of mindfulness will help you feel more connected to your own spirit—and the universe at work around you.

PARTICIPATE IN A RELIGIOUS STUDENT GROUP

It's often much easier to ask questions and talk about different topics when there aren't intimidating authority figures looming overhead and leading the conversations. In a student-run religious group, you can practice fellowship in a supportive environment, discuss your beliefs with other people who are at the same stage in life, learn more about a religion, and participate in community projects. Some groups might also offer special events focused on worship, as well as seminars and even movie nights. Most colleges have tons of student-led spiritual organizations across all faiths, so explore which one might be a good fit for you. You may also find groups specifically designed for certain students—like athletes practicing Christianity, women who follow Hinduism, and more. Joining one of these groups lets you get involved on your campus in a meaningful way.

TRY A YOGA CLASS

Yoga involves much more than putting on those stretchy pants and getting into Tree Pose. It's a spiritual exercise in mindfulness—using different physical poses and breathing exercises to clear your mind and usher in positive energy. And it can be a fantastic workout!

From homework to friends to family, you're constantly getting pulled in a million directions. You've got to finish that essay! But wait, friends are asking about grabbing dinner somewhere... Oh, and your parents are asking if you can visit home this weekend. It's a lot. And practicing yoga can help you feel grounded in the present, connect with the energy both within and around you, quiet your mind, and let go of control. It also teaches willpower, since you're combining intentional movement with getting your heart rate up, breathing deeply, *and* practicing awareness of the present moment. Plus, since you're constantly checking in with your thoughts, feelings, and emotions, you learn how to better listen to and trust yourself. Best of all, if you're not already part of a team or club on campus, it can be a great way to find a deeper sense of community at your school.

VISIT WITH A SPIRITUAL ADVISOR

Chaplains exist on campus to help you explore opportunities and resources related to spiritual development—whether you practice a religious tradition or not. Consider them an extra person in your circle of support: a spiritual mentor who can help you thrive at school. And you can go to a college chaplain for just about anything—not just a religious issue. You can visit a chaplain to vent in confidence about a difficult situation, to ask for help during a tough personal time, or to learn more about social justice or service groups (both faith-based and secular). Chaplains may also be able to provide assistance in navigating the different administrative elements of college, too, and put you in touch with other campus services that you didn't even realize existed. So, schedule a visit with your own chaplain, or pop in during open office hours to chat.

TALK ABOUT VOCATIONS WITH YOUR PEERS

"Will I get into a graduate program?" "Will I find a job after graduation?" "What am I supposed to do with my life?" You've probably already asked yourself these questions (or you are now!). While you can't map out all the answers to those questions, you can definitely start thinking about your vocation—that is, whatever you feel called to do based on your interests and values. Yes, the reasons for having a job also involve money, but what you get out of your work and how much you enjoy it depends hugely on whether you are genuinely interested in it and it falls within your set of beliefs. It is about fulfillment and a sense of purpose. And the best way to glean what will make you feel fulfilled in your future career is the spiritual journey you take to figure out just what your passions and values are.

Taking the time to ask your friends and classmates about what they find meaningful is an easy step in that journey to realizing what gives you purpose. Discuss how they are currently pursuing those passions, and think about how you might do the same.

COZY UP

"Hygge," a Danish word, refers to a feeling of contentment based on comfort. It's a way of life that encourages cultivating connections with others, enjoying what you have, and being present. Practicing hygge is a unique spiritual experience that tethers your body and soul to the universe around you—by getting cozy! You can try out hygge by hanging up string lights in your dorm room, sipping a mug of hot chocolate under a thick blanket during finals week, wearing warm socks and a big sweatshirt to the dining hall, or inviting friends over to watch a movie or play games. Anytime you're focused on being yourself and enjoying time spent with others—taking a break from your problems and reducing any sense of drama in your life—you're practicing hygge.

CREATE A PERSONAL MANTRA

Mantras are repeated sounds, words, or phrases intended to elevate your consciousness and positively impact your state of mind. You can whisper, chant, or silently recite a mantra—sort of like a prayer—to bring yourself back to the present, calm your nervous system, and quiet racing thoughts. Maybe you're struggling with body image recently after noticing your weight has fluctuated (the dreaded Freshman 15 strikes again!). When you recognize those negative thoughts creeping in, try a mantra! By repeatedly saying a mantra, you shift your mind-set toward a positive intention, something that feels seriously empowering.

You can try a popular mantra from a religion (like the Sanskrit phrase "Aham Prema," meaning "I am divine love," or the Hindu word "Om") or an inspirational statement like "I deserve love," "I can get through this," or "I am capable." Repeat the mantra as you inhale and exhale deep breaths; if thoughts pop into your head, put your focus back on the mantra.

DETERMINE YOUR TOP THREE VALUES

As you think about a future career, you might spend a lot of time considering which classes you like most and which you hate—but determining your core values is equally important. In fact, the two go together. Values guide your personal choices, represent what you stand for, and shape how you interact with others. Your values may be influenced by your religious beliefs, but they're not necessarily equated with them; your values can also impact how you set goals or make decisions, but they are not related to outcomes. Core values may evolve and change over time as you grow as a person, but ideally your values continually align with your actions. Figuring out your main values can help you decide what major to pursue, what clubs to join, and what type of career path to explore.

Take some time to list out what your top three values are. If you aren't sure, check out your school's career center or talk to an academic advisor about programs, exercises, or self-assessment resources (like personality tests) that can help you determine what these values are.

HELP SOMEONE

One hallmark of a meaningful life is being kind to others. It's not just about being a good person: being kind and helping people makes a difference in other lives too. And it creates a sense of purpose in your own life. In fact, helping people is good for your health all around; it releases endorphins in your brain, reduces stress, increases positive feelings, and promotes social connections. It doesn't have to be a big gesture, either—you can hold the door open for another student on campus, pick up an extra sandwich for your roommate, or text your younger sibling to have a great weekend. These acts of kindness make a real difference, and inspire the people you helped to pay it forward. Maybe seeing you hold the door open encourages other students to start doing the same more often, instead of tuning out the people around them as they go to and from class.

SET AN EVENING RITUAL

Rather than losing your evenings to homework assignments and mindless hours of scrolling though social media (until it's somehow already midnight—where does the time even go?!), set an intentional ritual so you can actually give yourself the time to unwind before bed. Start by blocking out 10–20 minutes of time between when you get back to your dorm and when it's lights-out. You can fill this time with whatever serves your spirit: praying, meditating, reading, stretching, a quick walk outside, listening to music, journaling. It helps to do something small and productive, too, such as making your bed, reviewing your class schedule or to-do list for the day ahead, or drinking a glass of water alongside your coffee. In the evening, instead of falling asleep with your phone in your hand, give yourself ample time to decompress. Shut down the screens (yes—tablets, TVs, and smartwatches included) and spend a little time unwinding with a prayer or reflection. You can give thanks, release fears after a long day, send good vibes to someone you care about, or ask for guidance. You might consider setting an intention for the next day, too, regarding how you want to show up to your classes and other activities as your most authentic self. When you create a ritual to end your day, it helps you stay centered and positive, as well as feel more rested and nourished.

LEARN ABOUT YOUR FAITH HISTORY

Part of knowing where you're going is learning where you've come *from*—so it's worth considering the traditions and beliefs of your family, as well as your individual experiences in the past. This history has shaped who you are now—and can play a huge role in who you grow up to be, especially during these formative first years of #adulting. (*Ahhhhh!* Okay, let's not panic...that much.) Do a little bit of research: is your religious experience thus far rooted in community, culture, rituals, and/or beliefs? Are they ones you've chosen for yourself, or ones handed down to you over the course of generations? Have you focused on organized prayer and services in the past, self-guided meditation, and/or community impact? Does your religion inform how you dress, date, eat, or spend your weekends? Paying attention to the ways in which you've already experienced faith can be a great tipping point for deepening your own personal understanding of what's important to you—whether these things line up with past traditions, or are completely new.

LIGHT A CANDLE

Candles symbolize light in the midst of darkness, and they're used in many religions as a part of ceremony or worship. Some faith traditions view candles, fire, and lamps as a mode of celebration related to deities, a ritual to connecting to the spiritual world, or a way to set an intention for spiritual reflection. You can light a candle to request healing or say a prayer—by yourself or with others. Candles in different colors can be lit for specific intentions, too, like lighting an orange candle to promote creativity during a writing assignment, or a pink candle to send love and good vibes to a struggling friend.

One disclaimer: your school may have an open flame policy, so you may need to bring your candle outside, or save it for off-campus housing. You can also use a diffuser or flameless candle instead, or see if your school offers any candle-lighting ceremonies.

SPEND TIME IN NATURE

Fun fact: you're made up of all the same things that make up the planet (carbon, oxygen, good ol' H_2O...). So in a way, spending time in nature aligns you with what's already true about yourself. You're accustomed to days chock-full of classes, plans with friends, and maybe even a part-time or work-study job—not to mention all of those hours spent in front of a screen (hey, it's not your fault every professor seems to love essays), so getting outside in nature will feel extremely restorative and soothing for your spirit.

Spending time in nature not only reduces stress and inflammation in the body—it can also lead to a stronger relationship with the world around you. For example, walking in the woods beyond your campus and daydreaming while staring up at the clouds promotes a connection to the natural beauty of the world...which you likely miss when racing to class and frantically searching through papers for that assignment you hope you remembered to put in your bag.

PROMOTE BALANCE WITH AMETHYST

You've got a huge class load, multiple friends all wanting to do different things this weekend, a work-study schedule to plan around, and your mom is calling for the second time about when she will be able to visit. Okay, so how do you balance it all without losing some (read: most) of your sanity in the process? Answer: a little personal self-care. And that's where the amethyst can come in. This highly spiritual crystal is full of balancing energy; it rids the mind and body of negativity, soothes emotions, and can even curb overindulgence (maybe you can resist that fourth slice of pizza after all). Plus, it looks cool, so you can decorate your dorm room with it, or wear it in a necklace, ring, or bracelet to carry those calming powers with you to that next final exam.

ATTEND AN INTERFAITH EVENT

No matter what you believe, attending a multi- or interfaith event on campus is a great way to learn about different faiths. Some multifaith events might honor certain religious holidays or festivals, giving you the chance to observe ones that differ from your own faith tradition. These are also great opportunities for learning and socializing. Other events might focus on bringing different traditions together to break down "us versus them" attitudes, like when Jewish, Catholic, and Muslim students come together for open dialogue and a deeper sense of community.

When checking out a multifaith event on campus, you'll be encouraged to explore how people of different religious identities can learn from each other—promoting diversity, acceptance, understanding, and respect. Your college might even have a multifaith center through its campus ministry department, with rooms available for prayer, meditation, reflection, and conversation. Or you can see if any multifaith clubs exist to bring together students of different spiritual backgrounds on a more regular basis.

TRY ACUPUNCTURE

Acupuncture is an ancient Chinese natural health approach intended to heal by removing energy imbalances (or "blockages") in the body. An alternative spiritual practice, it uses tiny needles placed in specific areas on the body to, for example, relieve acute or chronic pain, reduce insomnia, improve mood, and promote mental clarity.

When your days are full of stressful assignments, long classes, fights with roommates over who should clean the bathroom next, and, of course, the occasional (well, not so occasional) all-nighter at the library, this can really come in handy. And don't worry: those little needles are so small that you'll hardly feel a thing (except for the healing effects, of course!). Meet with a trained acupuncturist to see if acupuncture makes sense for you. You can also learn more online, from where to find a great acupuncturist near your school, to what other benefits it can offer.

LOOK AT YOUR ASTROLOGY CHART

You've probably been asked, "So what's your sign?" before—but astrology goes way deeper than that. In fact, your Sun sign (what people are talking about when they ask about your "sign") is just scratching the surface. Astrology is the study of how cosmic objects influence your life. It uses the position of things like the sun, stars, moon, and planets to predict major life experiences, current situations and decisions, and—via the specific time of your birth—your personality and future relationships. Astrology is a unique facet of spirituality that can serve as a tool for cultivating personal wellness—even if you're a little skeptical. Exploring your birth chart can give you insights into who you are and what you want to do after graduation. Because you've got a lot to figure out (while still passing organic chemistry somehow), a little cosmic guidance can be incredibly helpful.

CARE FOR A PLANT

Gardening is like a moving meditation: it teaches you about growth, change, patience, and the power of both roots and blooms. Plants hold fast to the cycles of life and death, so they can inspire spiritual exploration into both the meaning of and your beliefs about the afterlife—things you may already find yourself questioning in different classes, in conversations with friends, and on your own as you continue to grow. Plus, caring for a plant mimics the importance of caring for your own body; you need to give it sunshine, water, and extra TLC whenever you start to notice signs of depletion. Keeping any sort of greenery in your dorm room can also make you feel more relaxed during a hectic week, because it reminds you of the beauty around you. If you aren't too sure about your ability to keep things alive, you can start with a low-maintenance plant like a bamboo palm or aloe vera. Then, test your green thumb with an orchid or banana plant (bananas not included).

WATCH THE SUN RISE OR SET

When's the last time you woke up early for the sunrise, or ventured outside the library to watch the sunset? If the answer includes an occasion when you pulled an all-nighter to cram for a test, or that one time you stayed up late partying with friends, you may want to give it another try for a little spiritual self-care. Many religions have worshipped the sun for its healing properties: sunshine gives off peaceful energy, represents new beginnings, and paints the clouds with beautiful colors. It's also good for your body as a natural source of vitamin D that calms your nervous system, boosts metabolism, reduces anxiety and depression, and makes you feel energetic. Similarly, watching the sun set can be a mindful way to conclude the day, whether you're snuggled next to someone you love or taking a walk outside before diving into homework. Both put you into a reflective mood, connect you to the beautiful universe around you, and help you feel gratitude for your life.

CHAPTER 4
HONOR YOUR HEART: EMOTIONAL SELF-CARE

Friendships, classes, exams, dating, work-studies—you've got a lot going on. And that means a lot of feels. People are often taught that some emotions are "good" and others are "bad," but the truth is, each emotion plays a valuable role and impacts the way you think, act, and interact with others. When you pay attention to your emotions, you look out for things and people that threaten your sense of balance—like overcommitting to too many campus events in a single week or being around peers who bring you down. Emotional self-care is all about caring for your emotional needs—so that you can manage those feels in a healthy way.

Each of the self-care activities in this chapter will help you focus on tuning into your emotions so you can practice resilience, honor what supports your own emotional health, and express your feelings in constructive ways. You'll learn to compliment yourself, build a system of supportive friends and family members, and set healthy boundaries. As you practice emotional self-care, keep in mind that you know yourself best, and all emotions are valid.

SAY NO

It's easy to overcommit in the name of achievement: signing up for one more club, stretching a five-page paper into fifteen pages, staying up all night to complete an extra reading for a class. Unfortunately, it's also encouraged among your peers, as everyone seems to be competing for who is the busiest or the most exhausted.

Learning how to say no is one of the most vital acts of emotional self-care you can practice—it's a way of standing up for yourself, preserving your own energy, and making room for the things you need *and* want. Saying no to someone else means saying yes to yourself—because when you aren't listening to your needs and wants, you eventually reach emotional burnout. Easier said than done, of course. You've probably found yourself saying yes out of guilt, the desire to please, or the pressure to succeed. These are hard things to ignore! So if you're not sure how to start saying no, use your stress level as a barometer; if your brain feels like a web browser with too many tabs open, that's probably a sign that you've pushed past your limits. Fill up your schedule with what's important to you, and let go of the rest.

CALL A LOVED ONE

There's no one like your best friend—whether it's a high school buddy, Mom or Dad, or a sibling. They truly know you—and love you no matter what. They make you laugh, give you a shoulder to cry on, and remind you that you're not alone. They also celebrate your successes, lift you up when life gets challenging, and want the best for you. No matter what you're going through, whether it's landing an internship, failing an exam, or fighting with a roommate, calling (or texting or video-chatting) one of your favorite people helps you stay connected to your sense of self. You can be genuine, share secrets, confess mistakes; you know they've got your back and vice versa. Plus, they will know just how to make you crack a smile. So if you're struggling with a bad grade or on cloud nine after a first date, be sure to reach out to your BFF.

STAY IN

These years are the time to live it up and have nonstop fun—which is great, until you're worn out from a week of studying and classes and would rather stay in for a change. You might feel guilty, or pressured to still drag yourself out for a night off campus, but it's perfectly normal (and sometimes necessary!) to spend some nights not being social or "on" with other people. Rather than going to a party, campus event, or dinner with friends, hang out in your dorm when you feel like you need to recharge. Maybe you just chill out with a book, listen to music, or catch up on sleep. You might prefer to stay in with your girlfriend or boyfriend, or have a relaxing night on your own in front of the TV. Sure, it may not be as *Instagram*-worthy, but staying in is all about feeling good and giving yourself the emotional care you need.

GIVE YOURSELF A COMPLIMENT

It feels great when someone gives you a compliment, right? Well, those good vibes extend to self-compliments too! Giving yourself a compliment has an immediate impact on your attitude and overall self-esteem. Kind words, or just words of encouragement, help you feel confident in your own skin, believe in your abilities, and appreciate the person you are. Even though you may want to wait for others to acknowledge or recognize you, there's just as much (if not more!) value in looking to yourself for a pat on the back. After all, if there's one good opinion you need in life, it's your own. Self-compliments are especially important when you're constantly surrounded by new and challenging experiences—like failed exams, differences of opinion, and a change in major—that can shake your confidence and invite harmful self-criticism.

When paying a self-compliment, you can celebrate a big success, praise smaller wins, or just encourage yourself: "You look gorgeous today," "You did your best on that research project," "I'm proud of you for making the track team," or even, "You've got this!" Whatever you need to hear, go ahead and tell yourself.

ASK FOR HELP

You're facing new situations every day: balancing demanding classes with extracurriculars, being away from home, dealing with professors who push you to excel, living with roommates who can't seem to clean their dirty dishes—all of which takes a toll on your emotions. It's hard to know when and how to ask for help, particularly if you feel pressure to handle everything on your own. But asking for help takes strength and shows a brave vulnerability. Reach out to any staff member on campus, like your dorm resident assistant, to figure out what resources and support systems are available to you. Talk to your professor if you're struggling to keep up with assigned readings or exams; you can also join a study group, get a tutor, or make an appointment at your school's writing center. If you're worried about finding a summer gig or job shadowing opportunity, or have no clue how to make a resume, head to the career services office. Asking for help is smart—not a show of weakness; it allows you to get the support you need and deserve.

WATCH FOR RED FLAGS

From serious relationships to casual, fun hookups, love and romance is certainly in the campus air. And when a relationship is healthy, it's awesome; the entire journey of liking, lusting after, and loving someone can be both thrilling and satisfying. Your partner champions your goals and dreams—from current studies to those aspirations beyond graduation. And you both are capable and deserving of open, honest communication so you can grow independently and as a couple. However, if the relationship isn't healthy, neither you nor your partner will grow. And that's not fair to anyone. Luckily, there are red flags that can tip you off to a relationship that isn't serving your well-being. These red flags might include a lack of respect, controlling or jealous behavior, an inability to make you a priority, an obsession with previous relationships, a lack of emotional support, or excessive drinking or drug use. Most importantly, any sign of verbal, psychological, or physical abuse should be taken seriously. If you find yourself in a toxic situation, reach out to a trusted friend, family member, or campus counselor for support.

REFRAME COMPLAINTS

At some point (okay, more than the one, let's be honest), you'll want to complain about everything: a boring professor, getting closed out of a class you wanted to take, the cost of tuition, poor grades, the struggle to transfer credits, the awful weather, tasteless dining hall food, and your less-than-ideal roommate. And it's perfectly fine to vent once in a while (and enjoy airing out that negativity), but nonstop complaining can eventually do a number on your overall happiness.

So, what do you do? Flip the switch on those complaints! The next time you hear yourself saying you "have to" do something, change it to "get to," and consider what positive things can come from that less-than-fun task. For example, instead of thinking, "Ugh, I *have to* write this essay," reframe it as a chance to learn and express yourself: "I *get to* practice putting my thoughts to paper—and I may learn a few new things that will help me in the class." Mindful appreciation (versus irritation) will be quite the mood booster! Plus, it will be easier to do over time. Soon you may notice you rarely complain (or at least save the complaints for that midweek vent sesh with your pals).

ENJOY SINGLE LIFE

Being single—whether you just got out of a relationship with a high school boyfriend or girlfriend, or you have been riding solo for a while—gives you a unique opportunity to truly focus on yourself. You can sleep, study, work out, eat, and do whatever else you want, whenever you want, without prioritizing someone else. You can be wholeheartedly involved on campus through clubs, Greek life, or intramural sports, and get your homework done without the distraction of a significant other. Basically, you get to be selfish. And that's not a bad thing! Being selfish doesn't equal not caring about anyone else—it just means you can put your all into your own needs and wants. You can study abroad for a semester, flirt, and prioritize whatever is important to you. And if you choose to be in a relationship in the future, this time spent nurturing yourself will mean bringing a healthy you into the partnership. So make the most out of your time alone!

SURROUND YOURSELF WITH POSITIVE PEOPLE

These years are critical for personal growth. You learn how to be responsible in terms of getting things like homework done, how to balance friendships with personal needs and academics, and how to be independent. And you'll meet a ton of new people who can significantly influence how those experiences turn out. While you're in charge of your own emotions, the people you surround yourself with also affect your attitude: positive friends lift you up, while negative friends bring you down. Try to build friendships with people who support your goals, bring joy to your life, and genuinely want you to thrive. Skip the "friends" who criticize or limit your development. Look for people who are honest, kind, and comfortable being themselves; if you're not sure where to start, you can sign up for a club, sorority or fraternity, or activity like your college newspaper to find friends who have similar interests. Or you can focus on prioritizing current people in your life who care about your well-being and like you for *you*.

SEND A THANK-YOU NOTE

Okay, okay—yes, thank-you notes are something your mom always made you write for birthday gifts as a kid. But they aren't old-fashioned: they're a timeless sign of appreciation that can directly benefit you in college. In fact, saying thank you with a simple, heartfelt message in a card gives you a chance to reflect on how that person helped you, create and share positive vibes, and even strengthen your networking skills. You can write one for the person who supervised your internship over the summer, your boss at an on-campus job, the professor who wrote you a letter of recommendation, a friend who passed along a hot tip about a teaching assistant opportunity, or a mentor who took you out for coffee. Think of a couple of people who you'd like to say thank you to, and jot down a few lines in a nice card. It only takes a few minutes to make someone's day.

ENJOY ALONE TIME

Alone time doesn't mean being lonely. Sometimes it's nice to be alone, especially after a long day or week of challenging classes, because it provides time to focus on yourself and what you need: a hot shower, a good book, a journaling session, or maybe a quick run. You're constantly surrounded by people—from classmates to roommates, to the constant stream of campus tours—so take advantage of any opportunity to spend time with yourself. If you bunk with a roommate, try to plan out moments when you can each have the room to yourself. Find a bench to relax on while listening to music. Do your homework in a private study room. Alone time might feel unfamiliar at first, especially as you adjust to a more independent way of living at school, but it's a simple way to practice self-care.

BE MINDFUL OF THE COMPARISON TRAP

You may have heard social media described as a "highlight reel," and it's true: all the posts you see tend to display only the most picture-perfect moments of a person's life. When you're scrolling through your go-to accounts, these pictures and stories can take a jab at your own sense of worth or identity, so much so that you might start to compare yourself to friends, classmates, people from your past, or even total strangers. Witnessing a bunch of friends together at a party might cause you to feel lonely or left out (even if you were just busy that night), while seeing a posed or professionally edited image might lead to negative thoughts about your own body. Anytime you're using social media and start to notice that you are feeling bad about yourself or your life, it's time to log off for a bit. Think about why a certain post sparked a bad feeling, and remind yourself that social media is just one tiny and often glamorized view into another person's world.

BUILD A SUPPORT SYSTEM

Having a network of support is vital for your health and emotional well-being. After all, those relationships lift you up when you need it most (and between academic pressure, homesickness, and late nights, there can sometimes be a lot of need). Your support system might include family members, friends, and mentors—all of whom champion your academic success but also look out for you in times of stress. These are the people who give you practical guidance and advice, as well as comfort and love; they hold you accountable for your goals, listen to your hopes and fears, help you problem-solve, and know just how to make you laugh. As you meet new people in your classes and other campus activities, you'll probably widen or adapt your support system—but you can also rely on the friends and family members who've supported you thus far. Be sure to stay connected through phone calls, texts, emails, or video chats, because this network of support functions as your go-to resource for making it through all of the ups and downs. They'll be the ones reminding you to stay positive and work hard along the way, and they'll also be the ones there with you at the finish line (a.k.a the walk across the stage for your diploma).

WRITE DOWN FIVE WORDS THAT DESCRIBE YOU

Don't worry: this isn't surprise prep for a job interview. Learning how to describe yourself in a few key words is useful not only from a career perspective, but also as a way to reflect on your strengths, skills, and values as you grow over these crazy, awesome years. It builds confidence and offers an easy way to appreciate yourself. It also helps you focus on the type of person you want to become.

Start by writing down several words that you think describe you—anything that comes to mind. Then narrow down the list. You can also ask people who know you well to offer their thoughts. What they have to say may surprise you! Once you have your five words, envision them as your best attributes: the qualities you're most proud of. Keep the list somewhere you can reread it whenever you need a confidence boost or reminder to stay true to yourself.

SEE A CAMPUS COUNSELOR

Whether you're dealing with a short-term issue like stress over a current assignment, or a long-term issue like an anxiety disorder, you can take advantage of the free, accessible professional help available on your campus. You can go biweekly, monthly, or whenever you feel the need to; you can also explore phone or video sessions rather than in-person ones if you commute to classes. Everything you tell a campus counselor is confidential, so it's a safe space to share your feelings. And if you think you don't have time for therapy due to a busy school schedule, or assume you're not *that* stressed and can handle everything on your own, think again. You don't have to struggle alone, nor do you have to wait for things to get "bad enough" to reach out for help. Anything that is bothering you is deserving of a chat with someone who can offer guidance. Plus, common stressors like feeling homesick, worrying about grades, or arguing with your roommate can spiral into more serious issues. A campus counselor can teach coping skills and share more information for additional mental health resources—whatever you need.

SET A HEALTHY BOUNDARY

If you think of your emotions as a house, having no boundaries is like constantly leaving the door unlocked: anyone can walk in at any time. Establishing boundaries allows you to manage your time and energy based on what is most important to you. You put your mental health first in a respectful, intentional way to avoid burnout and toxic relationships. If a friend keeps asking for tutoring help and you feel frustrated because you are running out of time to focus on your own work, that's a sign that you need to set a boundary with that friend. And if you feel resentful or uncomfortable (maybe because you feel pressured to keep saying yes to helping that friend even though you really want to say no), that's another sign that boundaries are needed. Setting boundaries might feel a little harsh at first (especially if you tend to try to please everyone), but it's a necessary act of self-preservation. By setting a boundary, you are taking note of your limits, tuning into your feelings, and giving yourself permission to do what's best for you—even if that means disappointing someone else (there's a reason people always say that you can't please everyone!).

EMBRACE A MISTAKE

Spending too much money at the campus bookstore (okay, the new shirts *are* pretty cool), ignoring your boyfriend's calls, waking up with a major hangover, not studying for tomorrow's test—mistakes come in all shapes and sizes. And they're also a fact of life. Between all of the new experiences, challenging classes, and crazy-busy weeks, you're bound to mess up, move in the wrong direction, or spectacularly fail once in a while. While those experiences might hurt your sense of self-worth, they often teach you what *not* to do next time, which ultimately helps you grow. So when you do make a mistake (because you will, and it's okay!), look at it from that perspective. "Hey, it wasn't fun—but I learned something!" Be vulnerable about the fact that you're human, feel the resulting emotions with a healthy dose of compassion, and embrace whatever happened.

IDENTIFY EMOTIONAL TRIGGERS

Emotional triggers are the things that automatically make you feel uncomfortable, stressed, frustrated, or sad. Sometimes, these triggers are easily identifiable, like if you're used to being a top-notch student and get a terrible grade on a history test. Other times, they seem to come out of nowhere, such as breaking into tears when hearing a certain song (only to figure out it reminds you of that lost love from freshman year). There's no right or wrong definition of an emotional trigger, as it varies from person to person, and it doesn't necessarily matter if the perceived threat is "real." For example, let's say your significant other isn't great about responding to texts, and it bugs you. There's no "real" threat here, in the sense of, say, the real threat of that grizzly bear charging at you in the woods. However, what you're feeling is certainly real, and those feelings indicate that you need to have an honest conversation with your partner about expectations and communication styles.

If something bothers you, it bothers you: those emotions are valid, and there's no changing them or willing them away. What you *can* do is pay attention to what does trigger certain emotions. Consider how to limit or avoid exposure to those triggers. For example, you could turn off the radio or switch to a different tune if you're listening to a song that makes you feel weepy—and then remind yourself to maybe pass on the emo music until you're in a better emotional state. By being aware of a trigger, you can also think through how you might manage any painful feelings if that trigger is harder to avoid.

TREAT YOURSELF

When you're feeling the pressure of crazy deadlines and high expectations each semester, schedule in opportunities to treat yourself. You can treat yourself to anything that makes you happy: a power nap, your favorite takeout meal, a good book, a piece of candy, or a splurge item you've had your eye on for weeks. This simple practice of self-care gives your brain a little dose of dopamine—a.k.a. the feel-good endorphin. It also encourages self-compassion, showing you just how good it feels to be kind to yourself. Plus, it motivates you to keep up the good work. You know how puppies respond favorably to getting a treat every time they follow through on a learned behavior like sitting or going potty outside? Well, people aren't too different here: treating yourself for good behaviors such as finishing a homework assignment or going to bed early the night before a morning class serves as positive reinforcement to keep up those behaviors. So, what are you waiting for? Go treat yo' self!

DISTINGUISH YOUR INNER CIRCLE

Unlike a broader support system, your inner circle is a small list of people that will fluctuate more over the years depending on whatever chapter of life you're in. For instance, you might have had a group of besties in middle school, and then that group changed in high school, and now the list people you confide in most has changed yet again since you've got to college. That's perfectly normal, and your friend circles may continue to shift right through to graduation: you'll have friends of convenience (the girl you make small talk with in the dorm bathroom), friends of proximity (the guys you sit by in your humanities class), friends from your very first day (the people you don't really have anything in common with anymore, but are still friends with after bonding over how terrified you all were to start college), and then the people you vibe with the most. You'll turn to your inner circle to talk about anything and everything, so knowing who is in your corner can make you feel supported and secure during those more uncertain times.

DO A MENTAL HEALTH SCREENING

Things can feel pretty overwhelming at times—the class load, social calendar, extracurriculars, and friend drama, just to name a few. Experiencing a wide range of emotions is perfectly normal, but if you're worried you may be at risk for a more serious mental health issue, your school may have student screenings available for things like anxiety, depression, eating disorders, addiction, and more. These screenings are usually free and confidential, and they can help you determine whether you need further professional support or treatment. You can access them online in your dorm room, through a special event on campus, or by walking over to the clinic in your free time.

So if you're feeling sad all the time, are struggling to function on a day-to-day basis, are dealing with extreme mood or energy changes, or have recently gone through a traumatic life event, a mental health screening can begin the process to get the help and support you deserve.

GIVE A COMPLIMENT

Think about how you feel when you receive a compliment: amazing, right? Compliments also have a domino effect! When you tell someone you're grateful for them, or you appreciate something they did, you then see how that compliment impacts the rest of their day for the better. And it affects you, too: you walk away feeling positive about yourself and life in general. Spreading good vibes can make all the difference when hectic class schedules, mounting assignments, and social obligations are issues for everyone across campus.

Challenge yourself to give a few compliments one day—or every day if you prefer. Tell the person in your group project that you admire their organizational skills; write a note of congrats when your roommate lands a part-time job; voice your gratitude for a friend who always gives great advice. Notice how good it makes you feel to make other people feel valued.

LINGER IN NOSTALGIA

Even if you love your friends, your classes, and the beauty of the campus at this time of year, nostalgia for your high school days can still hit hard once in a while. And it's perfectly normal! You might miss your old friends as everybody is now going their own way, beloved teachers who championed you, or the pure joy of having fewer responsibilities. Or maybe you are feeling wistful for the person you were in high school: prom queen, football star, debate captain, or class president. Thinking back on these times can be bittersweet, but it's also a chance to think about what still matters to you and build that into new experiences on campus. Also, try to keep things positive. Look at old pictures from yearbooks or digital albums, listen to favorite songs from those years, or reconnect with high school friends to swap stories. Then, let those sentimental emotions go and focus on enjoying your college years, because one day you'll look back at them with nostalgia too.

FACT-CHECK A THOUGHT

Your thoughts are influenced by all kinds of things: friends, parents, professors, childhood experiences, current classes, social media. And sometimes it's hard to know which thoughts are true and which come from an assumption or fear. Certain negative thoughts can even play in your mind on a loop, and those mental patterns influence your emotions. For example, if you keep thinking about how you're not good at meeting new people—based on something you perceived on your first day of freshman year—you're probably going to feel self-conscious in social situations going forward.

Luckily, there is a better way. Instead, you can acknowledge the thought, then take a step back to ask yourself if it is true. Was that one awkward introduction really representative of how you are every time you meet someone new? Is there any evidence that it actually was awkward for the other person—or did you just feel awkward that day and perceive everything that happened as proof of that feeling? Fact-check these thoughts, and let go of the ones that aren't true and don't serve you.

CUDDLE AN ANIMAL

If you left a family pet behind during the move to your dorm, you already know animals can be a huge source of comfort and companionship. Studies have even proven that petting and cuddling dogs can directly reduce stress levels for college students in particular, as well as increase happiness and energy levels. Many colleges provide animal therapy programs right on campus to help students deal with loneliness or homesickness—and often organize special events during midterms and finals where puppies will be brought in for snuggle sessions. You can also visit or volunteer at a local animal rescue shelter, or even stop by a nearby park off campus to scout out any friendly dogs. And if you are looking for a long-term companion (and have the means to care for them), you can check with disability services or residential life departments to see if emotional support pets are allowed on campus.

WRITE A LETTER TO YOUR FUTURE SELF

Imagining your life in the future may be a regular part of your day-dreams already, but if you want to have a better shot at manifesting your goals, try writing a letter to your future self as a college senior or newly minted graduate. Think about romance, career aspirations, where you want to live, what kinds of experiences you want to have had by then, and so on. Be specific about what you hope for! Writing everything down in a letter to your future self helps you create a clear vision for what you want, and encourages you to take action now on those dreams. Keep an open mind, because life may turn out in some pretty unexpected ways, but do identify your priorities and be intentional about the type of person you aspire to be.

CELEBRATE A FRIEND'S SUCCESS

Every success—from scholarships won to the spot you snagged on the track team or that perfect presentation—will make you incredibly happy and, unsurprisingly, boost your emotional well-being. Supporting the success of your friends is also important, as it boosts their emotional health—and yours too. It creates a sense of optimism and abundance on both sides: when you watch someone you care about excel at a task or hit their goals, it feels energizing and inspiring to you, while having you celebrate their accomplishment makes that person feel even better about what they have achieved. And as you make connections in your program or field of study, you'll meet people who will be forever grateful and glad that you took the time to celebrate their wins in those studies—and will do the same for you.

LET GO OF AN OLD STORY

Walking onto campus on that first day is truly a breath of fresh air: no matter who you were up until that point, you get to start fresh. You can totally reinvent yourself if you're so inclined! Against a backdrop of new people, new settings, and new experiences, you can decide what type of person you want to be—and you can choose to let go of any old narratives that no longer serve you. Everyone holds onto stories from the past, and sometimes you can get stuck on ones that feel particularly hard to shake. But now you can press the reset button on anything that limited or betrayed your sense of self. You can focus on only the stories that encourage you. If you were the class clown in high school but want to be taken more seriously now, go for it! If you feel like you can't pursue an accounting major because you've always been bad with numbers, think again: it's time to change that narrative with a little tutoring. The more you let go of outdated, restrictive stories, the more you create space for stories that help you grow and feel confident.

REDIRECT ENVY

It's completely normal to feel envious of friends once in a while. Who doesn't get that twinge of jealousy when a friend gets the only A on a hard exam? This is especially true if they are excelling in an area you feel insecure about. Maybe your roommate comes from a wealthy family and consequently doesn't have to worry about student loans—meanwhile, you're stressed about paying for tuition and balancing a part-time job with your heavy homework load. Or maybe you experienced jealousy when a friend made the school soccer team and you didn't. It's always tricky when someone else gets what you wanted, but when you feel that tug of inferiority or resentment, it can take a toll on your emotional health if left unchecked.

Try redirecting those emotions to a more positive place. Trust that there's enough to go around, and focus on being your best; channel that energy into your own priorities versus obsessing over what other people are doing. Even though envy often seems like a purely negative emotion, it can serve as a motivation for self-growth. It shows you where you can improve or what's important but currently lacking in your life.

PRACTICE SELF-AWARENESS

A major part of emotional self-care is simply paying attention to your feelings—from what kinds of situations spark certain emotions, to how you react to those emotions. You aren't nitpicking your faults or fixing what's "wrong" with you; you're simply getting curious about your emotions and how you express them, and noticing any patterns or habits that might be getting in the way of your success. These really are formative years, and the thoughts you start to reinforce at this stage in your life can easily stick around for years to come—so make sure they're helpful ones!

You might start this practice by thinking back to what kinds of things made you happy or mad or sad during high school, and how you reacted to those feelings back then. Then, contemplate whether anything has changed or stayed the same—either in your feelings or how you react to them now. You can write down the things you're good at when it comes to self-expression, along with what you want to get better at. You can even ask a friend to do the same for you, then compare the lists; you'll receive open, objective feedback that helps you grow.

BUY YOURSELF FLOWERS

You probably think of flowers as being reserved for special occasions like Valentine's Day, birthdays, and maybe when you graduated high school. But you can also buy a bouquet to give yourself a little pick-me-up anytime you need an emotional lift. Fresh flowers smell good, look pretty, and invite a sense of new life and positivity—which can be the perfect antidote to homework stress or a difficult exam. You can keep a vase in your dorm room or off-campus apartment to cultivate a regular habit of showing yourself some love. Group projects, reports, campus events, work-studies, keeping up with laundry and a shared bathroom that never seems to stay clean—you've got a lot on your plate! And you deserve to treat yourself to a little beauty. It can be a perfect motivational boost, too, since it's a nice reward for all of your hard work.

TAKE A MENTAL HEALTH DAY

Sometimes you have to miss a class if you're not feeling well. But what about the days when your body feels fine, but your emotions need a little TLC? This is when taking a mental health day can be just what you need. It helps you recharge, catch up on sleep, improve your mood, and give your brain a little break from all of the studying and homework. You can use the day to do everything that's been on the back burner lately: yoga class, meditating, a favorite hobby, or just a date on the couch with the TV. If you tend to be a type A person, you might view mental health days as a waste of time. After all, they just get in the way of doing what you need to do, right? Actually, taking a little time off from your busy routine can do wonders for productivity later on. Enjoying a mental health day every once in a while (you don't want to do it all the time, of course) leads to better stress management, a more relaxed mind-set, and a better mood, all of which support hard work once you're ready to hit the books again.

HAVE A GOOD CRY

Relentless finals prep, a long-distance relationship, class at the crack of dawn, hours of homework (and no clear progress): sometimes it gets to be a lot. And it can even leave you in tears. While society can sometimes label people who cry as weak or overly dramatic, crying is a completely natural way to express your emotions and react to stress. There's no need to be embarrassed or hold back if you need that type of outlet—whether it's because of a failed test, breakup, annoying roommate, or overwhelming homework load. Some experts even argue that crying has the power to *reduce* stress, as the physical act releases endorphins that improve your mood and ease pain. Bottling up your emotions when you're sad, frustrated, or angry takes a toll on your emotional health over time—after all, you can only ignore it for so long. So rather than trying to tough it out, let yourself have a good cry to wash those feels away (literally!).

VENT TO SOMEONE YOU TRUST

Some days are just plain tough, and when you're facing upcoming project deadlines, difficulties in managing homework and family obligations, and a demanding social life, you may need to blow off steam once in a while. Venting to a trusted friend or family member is great stress relief—plus, they can serve as a sounding board for any problems you're stuck on. Of course, the goal is to let go of negative emotions and then move on with a calmer, more positive mind-set, so make sure your venting doesn't shift into gossip or become a way to avoid the problem. Confiding in the right person helps you get a grip on your feelings, refresh your perspective, and think more clearly about whatever's going on. The person listening is a bit more removed from the situation, so as they listen to you, they might also be able to offer an objective opinion that sheds new light on things.

COVER YOURSELF WITH A WEIGHTED BLANKET

A weighted blanket, also called a "gravity blanket," is a heavy blanket—usually weighing from a couple of pounds all the way up to 30 pounds (depending on your body weight)—that promotes a feeling of security. It's just like being hugged or swaddled like a baby! The benefits of using a weighted blanket include better sleep, a calmer attitude, and reduced anxiety. It isn't going to necessarily zap your insomnia entirely or treat depression, but it can definitely minimize stress during a crazy week of exams and group projects, and help you sleep longer and deeper so you're not struggling to keep your eyes open during class. So if you have a noisy roommate making it hard to fall asleep at night, stayed up too late video-chatting with a friend from home, are thinking about a tough test coming up, or are feeling homesick for your mom's chicken noodle soup, slip under a weighted blanket. It's also perfect for a power nap between classes!

ADD POSITIVITY TO YOUR MORNING

Sometimes emotional resilience is needed to combat the negative images or messages you might encounter—like cultural narratives around not showing emotion, or being a certain size, or succeeding at any cost. One way to create this resilience is to give yourself a daily reminder of the things you want or choose to believe. A positive note on a bedroom or bathroom mirror you use every day can help kick that negative or self-critical voice to the curb; you can write down personal affirmations like "You are worthy," "You are amazing, inside and out," or "You've got this!" or daily resolutions like "Be kind," "Help others," "Remain grateful," or "Prioritize your health." Repeat the words in your head a few times whenever you look at the note to commit to those positive mantras or lessons. Reading these empowering words as you look at your reflection will help you focus your thoughts and emotional state on how you want to feel. If you don't have a mirror, put the note in your class planner, on the back of your phone case, or beside the mouse pad on your laptop.

BELIEVE IN A BETTER TOMORROW

You probably know someone who always seems to maintain a "glass-half-full" mentality no matter what happens. And you might wish you could handle your own failing grade or fight with a friend the same way. It feels unfair at times. But optimism is a learned skill, not something you're born with—which means it's a muscle you can flex to make stronger. It's all about choosing a helpful explanation for whatever is happening—one that allows you to grow and look at the bigger picture. For example, if you do poorly on a test for your honors class, you might assume it means you're not smart enough to be in the class at all. You end up feeling bad about yourself, hopeless about the class, and ready to give up. Instead, you can exercise optimism by looking at it as a specific incident that can be overcome with a bit of extra work. After all, it's a challenging class! Studies show that people who are optimistic experience better health, improved work performance, and for students in particular, higher grades. It is good for your emotional health not just while you're in school, but also whenever you face a setback.

CHAPTER 5
FIND YOUR PURPOSE:
PROFESSIONAL SELF-CARE

Professional self-care is all about finding a good sense of balance between working on current academic pursuits and planning for your career beyond graduation day. For you, that balance may mean discovering work that gives you a sense of purpose through a credited internship, figuring out how you can add value to an employer or industry by shadowing someone in your field, or meeting with a campus career counselor to discuss switching majors. It takes a lot of energy to actively plan for your future while experiencing everything college has to offer, and it's important to create good self-care habits so you can reach your professional goals—without burning yourself out.

This chapter covers easy ways to network like a pro, maintain good study rituals, get focused when that urge to procrastinate comes knocking, step out of your comfort zone, and set realistic goals. You'll learn new skills, navigate your finances, stay organized, and follow your passions. Practicing professional self-care will better equip you to dream big when it comes to your postgraduate path, and take the necessary steps to see those dreams through.

INTRODUCE YOURSELF TO SOMEONE NEW

Having an impactful first impression and cultivating good relationships are both important for a successful career in any field. And from living with a roommate to joining an intermural sport, there are tons of opportunities to practice these skills right on campus. You'll have the chance to introduce yourself to someone new pretty much every day, whether you're saying hello to a professor you haven't met before, getting to know the people living on the same floor of your residence hall, or starting a conversation with the person who sits next to you in class. Not sure what to say? Start with a friendly greeting, compliment their awesome shoes, or even joke about something that happened in class. You can even rely on small talk at first, like "It's crazy how nice the weather has been lately!" or "I heard this class was tough; do you know anything about it?" Then ask them questions to keep the conversation going (after class, of course), like what their weekend plans are, what they are majoring in, or where they are from. The more you practice introducing yourself, the more your confidence around new people will soar!

GET RID OF CLUTTER

It's pretty hard to study in a messy room. Even if you aren't exactly a neat freak, research shows that the extra stuff around you competes for your attention, making it harder for you to sift through information, go back and forth between tasks or assignments, memorize facts, and overall stay focused on your work. A simple form of self-care, decluttering your space helps your mind follow suit. Get rid of everything you don't want or need anymore, like random T-shirts from orientation that you never wear, broken pens, old receipts, travel mugs that are missing a lid, and the stuff you grabbed in the student life office because it was free but don't actually use or even want all that much. If you have random papers all over your desk, make digital copies of everything and then recycle the originals. You have limited surface space in your dorm room as it is, so try to keep things as clear and open as possible so you have room to think and work. You can also use storage containers with drawers, hooks on the wall, or under-the-bed storage for more space.

DEVELOP A STUDY RITUAL

Studying well means having a routine. Think about it: it's hard to get things done when you are being as spontaneous about doing your work as you are about what you and your friends are doing next weekend. We're all creatures of habit, but those habits require a little intention, structure, and diligence—especially at the start. Think about your current obligations, class schedule, and personality so you can make a plan that is ideal for *you*. Maybe you only have afternoon classes, and you're also a morning person, so studying first thing in the morning after taking a shower is best for you. Or, you finish classes earlier in the day, leaving plenty of time to spend the afternoon at a big table in the library with a pair of noise-canceling headphones. You may have certain days of the week with no class at all, so you can devote those days to studying in the comfort of your own room (and pajamas). Whether you always do jumping jacks beforehand, drink the same type of tea, or listen to a certain type of music, it doesn't really matter what your routine is, so long as you try to do the same thing every time to get yourself in the zone and stay focused.

DO SOMETHING TERRIFYING AND EXCITING

Breaking out of your comfort zone can be pretty scary—but it can also be exciting! And from the first day of orientation week, right up to graduation day and beyond, it's important to continually push yourself to do things that stoke your inner passion, even if you're a little terrified at the same time. For example, maybe the experience of coming to college in the first place made you feel nervous about living in a new place, being away from home, and doing well in classes—but simultaneously, you felt thrilled to explore a new city, meet new people, and grow. Instead of giving in to the more nervous thoughts, you were courageous—and it has paid off and will continue to do so. When new opportunities and challenges arise, saying yes to the excitement and "you've got this!" to the fear helps you go after what you want and broaden your horizons. And over time, you'll start to realize that getting outside of your comfort zone in this way makes life much more interesting.

GET A PART-TIME JOB

Need extra cash and have the time in your schedule? Working while in school is a great opportunity to garner some real-world benefits: extra income, better time management skills, more experience in the workplace—all of which will set you apart from your peers when you're job hunting later on. Of course, you'll need to practice good self-care habits to avoid burnout when working part-time: be sure to prioritize your studies to keep your GPA up, and try to find a job that complements your academic efforts, such as a research assistant or campus tutor.

Working through college also gives you a chance to meet new people and expand your social circles. Plus, you can make connections that help you in your career down the road. Some part-time jobs that tend to be flexible and have student-friendly hours include peer tutoring, babysitting, retail, and waiting tables. Other options include on-campus jobs like working at the bookstore, student union, rec center, or campus offices.

SET A REALISTIC GOAL

Become a CEO, live in a three-story house, retire early—you've got big dreams. And you should! Whether you want to graduate a semester early, get your master's degree, or land a competitive job right out of college, the sky truly is the limit. However, these major aspirations can also be a little overwhelming to think about: Where do you even start? How do you get from graduate to CEO?

That's where setting realistic goals comes in. It's not about squashing your dreams; setting realistic goals means making those big aspirations easier to achieve by breaking each larger goal into smaller, realistic steps or "mini-goals." This makes those dreams less overwhelming and helps you measure your progress through milestones that you check off on a daily, weekly, or monthly basis. For instance, if you want to start your own business, begin by outlining all of the supporting goals that are involved. This can include learning how to write a business plan, considering startup expenses, crafting a saleable elevator pitch, and branding your concept. Accomplishing each smaller task keeps you on the path to attaining that bigger dream.

GET TO KNOW YOUR PROFESSORS

It's easy to see a professor the same way you saw teachers in grade school: they are the "adult" and you are the "kid." They teach you class topics, then you go home. Having to talk to them after class just means bad news...right? Not anymore! You are an adult now too. And your professors are there for more than grading papers and giving lectures. So put in the effort to get to know them. Introduce yourself and tell them what you like about the class so far, or what you're hoping to learn; ask questions, chat about upcoming campus events, and even visit during office hours to become a familiar face. Reach out via email or phone for help with assignments when needed so they know you want to succeed in class. Get to know them as a person, too—not just as a professor: their background, interests, and life experiences. Not only can you learn new things beyond the class materials, but you can also get great recommendations for research or internship opportunities in your field of study. They may even help you find new opportunities you hadn't thought of before.

PLAN YOUR SCHEDULE WITH AN ADVISOR

Everyone is assigned an advisor at the start of freshman year to help with course selection and make sure degree requirements for a chosen major are going to be met. But did you know you can also look to your advisor to help explore different interests, look into class or major changes, or just talk about issues that have been stressing you out in your studies? You can also revisit your advisor any (or every) semester to make sure you are still on track and don't accidentally miss important classes or take ones you don't actually need. Things change—maybe you aren't passionate about science anymore, or you want to study abroad next semester instead of in two years—and your advisor is there to help! Take advantage of their open office hours and make appointments beyond what is required before course selections, so you can ask specific questions, let them know if you're having trouble with a class, or look into tutoring options or group study sessions. Your advisor is another important person in your college support system who can advocate for you and help you manage any academic stress.

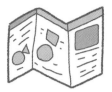

CREATE A VISION BOARD

When you envision a goal, you're more likely to achieve it, right? Well, creating a visual board that represents your short- and long-term objectives is an easy way to not only picture those goals, but also hold yourself accountable for them. It's also a daily creative reminder of where you're headed: inspiration in picture form! You can use a piece of cardboard or bulletin board to create a physical vision board, or check out a vision board app like VISUAPP or iWish if you don't have the space in your dorm room (or just want something you can carry with you everywhere). From there, you have complete freedom to put whatever you want on your board: pictures of things that motivate you, beautiful sketches or pages torn from a magazine to show what you want in your future, names of places you want to visit, quotes that inspire you, or anything else that speaks to you or represents your bigger dreams. Give yourself a solid couple of hours to get your board going, and then add to it whenever the mood strikes.

TAKE AN ELECTIVE CLASS

In addition to required courses, electives are a chance to explore your interests, broaden your knowledge related to personal or professional goals, and make your education more well rounded—which is appealing to employers down the road and beneficial to your own growth. You may have to take that History 101 class (a total snooze-fest since you couldn't care less about memorizing boring dates), but you get to follow it up with a fun graphic arts workshop—which is worth staying awake through the Revolutionary War slideshow. You can explore a topic you know little about, like children's literature or game theory, or a subject you're passionate about outside of your degree program, like cinema, painting, or dance. Talk to your advisor to see which electives fit your schedule without taking away from your major requirements. Whatever you choose may complement your professional goals—for example, taking a public speaking course as a marketing major. Or you can just have fun with it, like taking a guitar class so you can learn to play.

UNDERSTAND YOUR STUDENT LOANS AND FINANCIAL AID

Unsubsidized loans, interest rates, consolidation, grants, net price—there's a lot behind the scenes when it comes to student loans and financial aid. It almost sounds like a different language! And as intimidating, confusing, or downright boring as it all might sound, it's important to understand these aspects of education. After all, college is a big expense, and one that may impact your finances for years to come. Start by reading through any and all paperwork you receive so you know the details of any financial aid package, as well as loan interest rates and repayment schedules for your loans. You can work with your school's financial aid office to get assistance with budgeting, estimate your school expenses, address eligibility policy requirements, or figure out grants and work-study options. And as for federal or private student loans, a financial aid officer can help you plan accordingly, understand all that student loan lingo, and do what you can to lower the amount you owe—such as paying down interest while you're still in school to save money in the long run.

JOIN A CLUB

Whether you're looking to learn more outside of class, make new friends, or just enjoy a favorite hobby, clubs are a fun (and free!) way to get even more out of college. French club, chess club, drama club, Quidditch club (yes, it's a thing)—there's something for everyone, no matter what year you're in. And your university probably has an activity fair at the start of every school year so you can check out everything that's available. Common clubs are oriented around sports, volunteering, Greek life, specific academic departments or fields, hobbies, and the arts. From cooking club to glee club, you can make connections to great resources, programs, and people, practice your leadership skills, and try something new in the process. Being involved in an activity you enjoy is good for your well-being, gives you a break from studying, and opens doors to all kinds of things that can influence your career down the road.

MAKE YOUR SPACE FEEL LIKE HOME

There really is no place like home, and when it comes to college, it's up to you to make your room feel homey. True, you can't repaint the walls or make the window larger (or else you'll get hit with a fine!), but you can decorate it however you want. And your room and the overall vibe of your living situation can seriously affect your day-to-day experience: bare walls with fluorescent lighting and a plain college-issue mattress doesn't exactly scream sanctuary, you know? So do what you can to make it feel more like home. Put up colorful posters or art prints, add photos of your family or pets to the nightstand and desk, hang string lights, top the bed with extra pillows and a soft comforter, and roll out a cozy rug. You have complete control over how you want your dorm room to look and feel (unless you have a dorm roommate—in which case make sure you both agree on the décor!), so make it your own. With the right home space, you'll be set for success.

HONE YOUR LEADERSHIP STYLE

Leading is a big part of success in any job post-graduation. Whether you go on to be an editor, shift supervisor, or CEO, you're going to be leading at some point in your career; from one client, to a small group of employees, to a whole company, leading is leading. Learning how to lead others definitely takes time, but luckily, all of those class credits mean plenty of chances to practice. You should also pay attention to the leaders you already admire, either at your school (professors are leaders too!), in peer-to-peer settings (projects that another classmate leads), or back home (the boss at your part-time job in high school, for instance). Observe what they do and don't do, and take note of what you'd like to emulate in your own leadership style. You can also read books or articles, and even listen to podcasts about leadership. The point is, everyone has their own individual style when it comes to leading others, so use this time to get a leg up on figuring out your own. You can also ask for feedback from those who know you best.

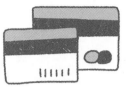

KNOW THE PROS AND CONS OF CREDIT CARDS

Ah, the credit card: just swipe a plastic card through the checkout and those new shoes are paid for you! Well, not exactly. You still have to pay, just in smaller amounts over time versus everything up front at the cash register. Credit cards build up your credit score for significant purchases later on, like renting an apartment or buying a car, and they're great for emergencies or unexpected expenses, such as a new laptop, flight home, or emergency room visit. But there are also cons and restrictions to remember when you use a credit card: hefty late fees, credit limits, high interest rates that can skyrocket your balance if you aren't careful, and that temptation to spend money you technically don't have—which can be a real problem if you're unable to pay a bill regularly or on time. Don't let that scare you, though. Managing one or two credit cards can teach you how to pay off a balance, build your credit score, and pay attention to your financial habits. One way to stay accountable? Put less on plastic than into your savings account.

MANAGE A GROUP PROJECT

Before you groan and write off group projects as the worst thing ever, consider this: they're actually a great way to learn how to collaborate with other people effectively. And that's a skill you'll put to use nonstop in the working world—no matter what industry you're in or job you might have. From time management to communication strategies, group projects teach you how to manage conflict, share ideas, set roles, track goals, and schedule meetings. You experience what it's like to work in both small and large groups, over the course of a couple weeks or an entire semester, and figure out how to play to everyone's strengths, including your own. Maybe you naturally gravitate toward organizing all the group members, or creating the design of a presentation, or digging deeply into research. Once you've noticed these skills, you can then apply them to other courses or assignments to keep developing them and eventually use them in your career.

LEARN HARD AND SOFT SKILLS

Certain majors or careers are heavy-handed on either hard or soft skills. What exactly does this mean? Well, engineering, medicine, and accounting—for instance—will always require technical knowledge (hard skills) first and foremost, while fields like sales, teaching, and public service often need more emphasis on communication (soft skills). Regardless, you'll need both at some point—after all, employers want people who can toggle between the two worlds. Plus, having both will help you navigate situations throughout your life, from the classroom to the workforce, to even your personal world. Learning how to make tables in Excel is just as valuable as learning how to influence peers with an argument. (Hey, eventually you're going to need to keep track of all of those monthly bills and student loan payments.) Similarly, how you handle criticism matters as much as those programming skills. For example, even if you're excellent at project management planning in your post-graduation job, you'll have to be equally good at handling constructive feedback from clients. You'll likely learn the hard skills you need for your career through your classes, but also look for opportunities to continually boost your soft skills, such as being an RA or teaching assistant, leading a student organization, or freelancing for a local paper.

OPEN A SAVINGS ACCOUNT

Saving money is probably the last thing you're thinking about—you're trying to live it up and eat more than just ramen noodles for every meal, after all. However, opening a savings account doesn't require a lot of money, and it gives you a baseline to build positive financial habits. Look for a local bank that caters to college students, as they'll typically offer options such as no-fee ATMs, free online banking, free bill pay, and more. You can set up an automatic savings plan to move small amounts of money to your savings account each week—for instance, if you save $10 a week for a year, that's over $500! You can also check out investment apps such as Chime or Qapital, which round up your purchases to the nearest dollar and put that sum in a savings account for you. When you prioritize saving money, you can lessen any financial burdens while creating a nice nest egg for emergencies and expenses, both in school and after graduation.

SEND A COLD EMAIL

You already anticipate networking after graduation, but you can practice before then too. This will make it less intimidating when it comes time to reach out as a graduate, and it also sharpens those communication skills for any professional situation. Start with your university's career office. Ask them to connect you with anyone who graduated with a degree in your major and/or works at a specific company you are interested in; you can also talk to older students in your program to see if anyone knows someone willing to talk to you. Once you find a lead, send a short email that outlines who you are, why you're contacting them, and what you're hoping to learn (or what you're requesting from them). Focus on a clear, small request, such as a 15-minute phone call to answer questions that you can even send in advance, or a coffee date to learn what it's like to work in a certain field. You might end up reaching out to friends of friends, siblings of peers, people you've met briefly in real life, or even complete strangers: you never know who can help you out. Don't take it personally if they don't respond (people get busy, inboxes get flooded with other more urgent emails—it's rarely personal!), and trust that over time you'll make helpful connections.

EXPLORE A STUDY ABROAD PROGRAM

You've heard that traveling is a life-changing experience—and it's not just a movie cliché: it's true! Traveling breaks down cultural stereotypes, broadens your knowledge, and helps you grow personally. It also gives you a professional edge, as employers are interested in people who are capable of taking on new challenges, getting out of their comfort zone, meeting different types of people, and learning new things. It really is a full-package deal—a unique chance to evolve professionally, personally, and academically—all while going on an awesome adventure! Your school likely offers different types of travel abroad programs, from language-intensive weeklong trips and summers in different major cities, to a full semester abroad at a sponsored university. Connect with your class advisor, or the study abroad office at your college, to learn more and figure out what financial and academic options work best for you. Traveling will completely open up your world!

JOB SHADOW

Job shadowing is like taking a glimpse into a specific field. You observe and follow a professional around for a short period of time to explore whether or not you want to pursue a career like theirs after graduation. It isn't the same thing as an internship, as you won't necessarily get hands-on experience, but it definitely helps you understand what certain jobs are like during a typical day. You can get a sense of a company's culture, and you can also ask that person questions such as what they like and dislike about the job and company, what are the challenges and rewards involved in the job, what advice they'd give someone interested in that career, and what type of training has proved most useful for them. To find someone to job shadow, reach out to your career center on campus to see if they have any programs you can apply to. You can also ask a professor in that field for leads, or do your own research on companies in the area before asking if job shadowing opportunities are available.

LEARN BASIC CODING

No, this isn't just for computer science majors or wannabe hackers. Computer coding is a skill that leads to better pay, improved logical reasoning and problem-solving, and more career options for anyone! It also translates across any field. Regardless of what career you go into, computer science skills are applicable—whether you are a nurse entering patient information into the hospital database, a business owner looking to revamp your company website, or an artist hoping to sell your work online. Many colleges offer specific classes for coding, so look for one that fits into your course schedule and workload. You can also check out tons of different online options and learn on your own time, at your own pace. And don't worry about your level of computer knowledge (or, more specifically, the lack thereof); beginner programs will walk you through step-by-step—starting from the most basic elements of coding.

DEVELOP AN ONLINE PORTFOLIO

Move out of the way, boring old resumes (well, not completely out of the way—you still need one for most job applications): the digital portfolio is here. A website devoted to you and your accomplishments, the digital portfolio is a great way to make a positive impression on prospective employers while telling the unique story of who you are and what your professional goals are following graduation. To build your portfolio, you can track all of the creative presentations you do for classes, upload academic work you're particularly proud of, post recommendation letters from professors, and even create blog posts about your academic progress. Think strategically about your audience in terms of what kind of information would be most useful to them, while also representing your very best work. Then, instead of carrying around paper resumes or cold-emailing files, you can send a link to make a much bigger impression.

VISIT A CAREER COUNSELOR

"How do I even start looking for a job?" "What should I bring to an interview?" "What do I actually want to do with the rest of my life?" (Insert panic here.) Okay, first take a deep breath—or ten. Now, to answer your questions: that is exactly what the career counselors on campus are there for! They can help you figure out a career path, find a job (either during college or after graduation), and give feedback on things like resumes, cover letters, digital portfolios, and business cards. You can get assistance for your specific needs, such as finding a summer internship on the East Coast, learning what someone might do with a philosophy degree, or calculating entry-level salaries. A counselor may also be able to coach you before an upcoming interview, or provide advice regarding what employers pay attention to on social media platforms. They can also point you toward specific campus resources, such as alumni contacts, speakers or workshops, job fairs or boards, industry news, or professional associations you can join. So, go schedule that appointment—and keep breathing!

TRY MORNING PAGES

Morning Pages, a creativity exercise originally coined in the book *The Artist's Way* by Julia Cameron, involves three pages of stream-of-consciousness writing done first thing in the morning—by hand and on paper. There's no wrong way to do Morning Pages: you literally just write whatever comes to mind until you've filled three pages. Don't stop even for misspelled words or run-on sentences (there are no grades given out afterward!). You don't need to be a writer or artist, either: the exercise isn't looking for award-worthy prose. The intent is to rid your mind of any negative self-talk so you free up mental space before focusing on your classes, assignments, and personal life. As a self-care practice, Morning Pages can help you unlock the steps to achieving your goals and identify new ideas. Plus, spending 15–20 minutes each morning writing down everything that pops into your brain can be a great way to relieve stress during a busy exam week, and provide a sense of accomplishment every single day.

TAKE A PERSONALITY TEST

Personality tests are designed to help you find the right path based on your strengths and weaknesses; they're not the be-all and end-all gospel, of course, but rather a reference point as you attempt to decide on a major, pick classes, and pursue jobs. Some research even shows that aligning your personality to your field of study can lead to better grades, a higher GPA overall, improved work performance, and increased job satisfaction.

On a more personal level, these types of tests can help you understand your best qualities and how to put them to use. For example, if you take a Myers-Briggs personality test and learn you're more of a "caregiver" type, you might now have a light bulb moment and think, "Oh, that's why I'm drawn to a nursing career!" That result can then give you insights into what strengths can be built on and what things can be improved to see those aspirations through. Some companies even use these kinds of assessments to vet applicants, so you may run into them again when you're looking for a job. Your school's career center may offer versions of different personality tests, and you can also find a ton of options online.

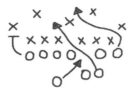

MEET WITH A LIFE COACH

Life coaching in college is different than therapy or career counseling. In fact, it's kind of like a hybrid of the two. Think of it as a more in-depth relationship that focuses on leading you from where you are now (in the professional and academic world and in your personal life) to where you want to be after graduation. You can meet with a life coach to get further clarity on your personal and career goals, create accountability habits (like texting a friend after you update your resume or paying to attend an online workshop so you don't bail at the last minute), receive an objective perspective on your decisions, and focus on personal development in ways that take you to the next level of success. If you're unsure of what to study, you're beginning to prepare for interviews, or you're planning for graduate school, a life coach can help you take the next steps (just like a career counselor), but also improve on more personal aspects of your life—like your self-confidence, individual values, and sense of purpose—that can impact your career success.

GET A TUTOR

Tutoring is like personal training for your studies. Rather than wait until you're struggling with a subject or falling behind in a class, you can work with a tutor to be proactive, get regular assistance and feedback on your work, and learn at your own pace. Tutoring helps you work through that more complicated or confusing course material and prioritize your time appropriately. Plus, individualized one-on-one sessions allow you to try different study techniques, walk through specific information in your textbook, and work on practice problems to improve your grades. And a nice bonus: this shows your professor that you're taking the class seriously and trying to do your best work, so they're more willing to work with you on lower grades or challenging assignments to ensure you succeed in the class. Your school likely has a student support or tutoring center with peer tutors who are particularly strong in a subject area. Working with a peer tutor can give you a sense of partnership when it comes to your studies—plus, these students are better equipped to address your frustrations because they've been in your shoes before.

WRITE A
PERSONAL STATEMENT

You probably wrote a personal statement for college applications and any scholarship considerations—but don't put that pen down just yet. A personal statement is also a great way to organize your academic and career goals, feel empowered, and even figure out the next steps toward success. Think of it as a way to tell the story of who you *are*, versus just what you have *done*.

Spend some time brainstorming what you want to say, then focus your statement on specific topics like what you're passionate about, why you're confident about your future, or how you made it through a difficult experience to come out stronger. For example, maybe you played sports your entire life and you want to major in physical therapy. What did those years teach you, and how would it apply to being successful in school or your career?

ATTEND AN EXTRA-CURRICULAR SEMINAR

Outside of clubs and organized sports, extracurricular seminars or lectures by campus professors or invited speakers are worth the second look. Workshops and seminars encourage insightful conversations and help you develop new ideas. Plus, attending these types of events can help you feel more connected to other students, your professors, and your school as a whole. Some professors will even provide extra credit based on your attendance at certain extracurricular events, as these experiences further your knowledge in the class—and overall. In fact, an extracurricular event can have a huge impact on your perspective or opinions in some pretty unexpected ways, so take advantage. Interested in a topic that isn't related to your own studies? You can also attend events outside of your department or program—the extra interest is more than welcome! Different seminars or lectures on campus can include poetry readings, political panels, historical films, personal experience lectures, and more.

ORGANIZE YOUR COURSE MATERIALS

Every class comes with a detailed syllabus chock-full of reading assignments, quizzes, test dates, and much more, so it's important to stay organized once a semester gets going. Be sure to have a planner (digital or paper—your pick!) to track homework, social plans, work schedules, and everything else you have going on, along with folders to keep all your class information and paperwork in the same spot. You can even color code your stuff for each class to help you visually keep it straight and find things quickly (yellow for math, since it's your least favorite color and least favorite subject, for example). Use your smartphone or a whiteboard or corkboard to track quick notes or reminders to yourself, and list out important dates on a desk calendar or calendar app. Also, take some time to read through the entire syllabus early on so you know what to expect, and consider combining all the key dates for every class into one master syllabus for yourself so nothing gets overlooked.

PRACTICE AN OPEN MIND

There's a real comfort in what's familiar. Family traditions, holidays, and long-standing beliefs are all taken for granted throughout the years. And up until college, childhood friends, teachers, and parents have all played a major role in your perceptions of the world—and yourself. But now, surrounded by tons of new people, new experiences, and a great deal of personal freedom, you encounter different ideas, beliefs, and cultures that may shape you in unexpected ways. Keeping an open mind is essential to your personal growth during this time. It may be a bit nerve-racking at first as you step out of a comfort zone, but when you welcome the unfamiliar in your journey, you can broaden your horizons, learn different ways of living, and explore other perspectives—all major parts of your success in every part of life. Instead of making assumptions, try to be curious about all viewpoints; one perspective doesn't have all the answers, and there's merit in admitting you always have more to learn. Whether it's people, beliefs, or activities—even food or music—practice an open mind.

APPLY FOR AN INTERNSHIP

Internships aren't just a great way to boost a resume! They are full of experiences and skills that will be critical in professional life after graduation. You get the chance to test out what it's like to work in an office, handle customers or interact with coworkers, and form relationships that will provide future job references or the foot in the door to a particular company or field. Think about your career goals, then research jobs in that field and note the ones that interest you. Businesses of all sizes partner with universities to create a pipeline for students, so work with your school's career center to find internship openings in whatever interests you. Internships are typically available during the school year, so you can work one into your class schedule for credits. Too many required courses on your plate? Look into a summer internship! Some internships even happen online, if that works better for your schedule. Even though many students do an internship in their junior and senior year to strive toward a full-time job offer, you can start looking as early as you like. You might even find one that's paid!

WATCH A DOCUMENTARY

Documentaries aren't reserved for class—and they don't have to be on boring topics that have you falling asleep, either. There are tons of different, interesting documentaries available online and on popular streaming services for whatever sparks your curiosity! You can discover something you wouldn't normally learn about in class, take a deeper look at different people, places, and lifestyles you have always wondered about, or check out topics related to your major, like crime investigations, fashion, or positive psychology. Documentaries are a fun conversation starter for your friends and classmates, and they can even change the way you think about certain things. Keep in mind that many documentaries are made to support or promote a specific viewpoint, so it's always worth verifying the accuracy of any claims made.

CONSIDER SWITCHING MAJORS

A lot of students enter college with an undecided major, and many will change their major at least once before graduating. Luckily, most schools don't require you to choose until the end of your sophomore year, which gives you plenty of time to try different classes, explore what you are interested in, and rack up those general education credits (you need them anyway). Of course, certain colleges or programs request early commitments because of the class requirements, but if you absolutely need to switch gears—you're in a pharmacy program, for instance, and you realize there isn't anything you'd rather do *less*—you can; it may just impact when you're able to graduate. At the end of the day, it's not worth suffering through a major if you're stressed out 24/7, are getting poor grades no matter how much tutoring or extra credit you get, or just aren't interested in pursuing a job in the field anymore. You might panic at first about the time and money you've already invested, but here's the thing: it's perfectly okay to change your mind—and trusting your gut is way better in the long run. Let go of any worries about switching your major, and work with your college advisor to create a new academic plan.

COLLECT INSPIRING QUOTES

When it's hard to find the motivation to get through that last essay paragraph or review chemical compounds for another hour, inspirational quotes can be the perfect tool for getting focused, pushing through a difficult assignment or situation, setting new goals, and staying both positive and confident. There's real power in words: they can offer wisdom and coaching in truly meaningful ways. And there's a quote out there for whatever you're going through—be it a shift in academic study, the most painstaking report in the history of academia, or a fight with your bestie. So when you need a boost, look online, turn to a favorite book, or even skim through a magazine for any quote that strikes a chord. You can also ask your friends or classmates if there are any quotes that have encouraged or uplifted them in the past. Write the quotes down in a little book, plaster them all over your dorm room walls, or save them in a Word document on your laptop to reread whenever you need inspiration.

LET YOUR CURIOSITY LEAD YOU

College is about more than memorizing information, building your resume, and getting that A. It's a unique time in your life where you have full permission (and the tools needed) to pursue knowledge in a wide variety of topics. Cultivating curiosity and a love of learning is crucial to getting the most out of your college experience while also developing marketable skills and gaining exposure to the professional world you will soon be joining.

Pay attention to what sparks your own curiosity—and explore it! If you like learning new things in science class, or enjoy musing over questions about different religions, follow those interests. Maybe you're obsessed with successful news anchors, and love listening to podcasts. Over time, those interests could translate into a career in media!

Soon enough, you'll be off on the next adventure in your life, so view college as your time to really think about what excites you, test those things out, talk about them with others, and find purposeful work.

INDEX

Acupuncture, 132
Affirmations, 115, 123, 174, 207
Alcohol use, 25, 39
Alone time, 103, 113, 141, 149
Astrology, 133

Beverages, 19, 22, 25, 39, 52
Blanket, weighted, 173
Body. See also Physical self-care
  balancing, 17–55
  energizing, 19, 24, 26, 29, 33
  exercising, 24, 33, 36–40, 44, 46,
    50–51
  nutrition for, 21, 27, 30, 32, 42, 47, 95
Boundaries, setting, 138, 154
Brain power, 11–12, 57–95.
  See also Mental self-care
Burnout, 83, 139, 154, 183

Candles, 128
Career counselor, 186, 202, 205
Career goals, 13–14, 121, 177–215.
  See also Professional self-care
Chakras, balancing, 109
Clothing, 54
Clubs, joining, 38, 94, 124, 131, 146, 190
Clutter, eliminating, 90, 180
Coffee/tea, 19, 22, 52
Comic books, 94
Comparisons, 150

Complaints, 145
Compliments, 142, 157, 160
Computer coding, 200
Control, releasing, 115, 119
Cooking tips, 32, 42.
  See also Foods
Counseling, 144, 153, 202, 205
Counting backward, 71
Credit cards, 193
Crying/sadness, 156, 159, 171
Crystals, spiritual, 130
Curiosity, 210, 212, 215

Dancing, 51
Daydreams, 84, 129, 164
Distractions, 59, 60, 78, 92, 105
Doctor appointments, 43
Documentaries, 212
Donations, 100
Dorm room, organizing, 180
Dorm room, personalizing, 191
Drug use, 25, 39

Elective classes, 69, 188
Emotional self-care
  alone time, 103, 113, 141, 149
  boundaries, 138, 154
  burnout, 83, 139, 154, 183
  comparisons, 150
  compassion, 157

complaints, 145
compliments, 142, 157, 160
counseling, 144, 153
crying/sadness, 156, 159, 171
describing self, 152
explanation of, 12–13, 138
friendships, 140, 147, 158, 165
homesickness, 151, 153, 163, 173
learning from mistakes, 64, 66, 155
mantras, 123, 174
morning routines, 49, 70, 174
nostalgia, 161
optimism, 164, 165, 175
pets, 163
positivity, 147–48, 151, 160–61,
   169, 174
red flags, 62, 144
redirecting envy, 167
saying no, 139, 154
security, 122, 158, 173
self-awareness, 168
self-confidence, 54, 152, 157
self-esteem, 31, 109, 142
single life, 146
stress management, 151, 153, 163,
   167–73
support systems, 143, 151, 158, 172
thank-you notes, 148
triggers, 156
Energy, balancing, 109, 130
Energy, boosting, 19, 24, 26, 29, 33,
   50–51
Envy, redirecting, 167
Essential oils, 112
Exercise, 24, 33, 36–40, 44, 46, 50–51

Eye care, 41

Feelings, 12, 137–75.
   See also Emotional self-care
Fight-or-flight instinct, 81, 86
Finances, 75, 167, 193, 195, 196
Financial aid, 65, 189
Flowers/plants, 134, 169
"Flow" state, 78
Foods, healthy, 21, 27, 30, 32, 42, 47, 95
Friendships, 85, 116, 140, 147, 158, 165

Gardening, 134
Germs, 23
Goals, 13–14, 164, 177–215
Gratitude list, 107
Gravity blanket, 173
Group projects, 160, 169, 173, 194

Help from others, 143, 151, 158, 172
Helping others, 100, 104, 125, 174
Homesickness, 151, 153, 163, 173
Humor, 75
Hydration, 19, 52
Hygge, 122
Hygiene, 23, 45

Illness, 23, 43
Inspiration, 87, 102, 123, 187, 214
Internships, 54, 117, 140, 148, 178,
   185, 211

Job, part-time, 183
Job shadowing, 199
Journals, 87

Leadership skills, 104, 190, 192, 194
Lectures, 39–40, 44, 67, 77, 185, 208
Letter to self, 164
Letting go, 66, 115, 139, 162, 166, 172, 213
Life coaches, 205
Loans, 75, 167, 189, 195
Lungs, caring for, 37, 73, 91

Majors, switching, 213
Mantras, 123, 174. See also Prayer
Massage, 28
Meals, 27, 32, 42, 47. See also Foods
Meditation, 71, 105, 112, 126–27, 131, 170
Mental self-care
    burnout, 83, 139, 154, 183
    comic books, 94
    counting backward, 71
    daydreams, 84, 129, 164
    drawing from memory, 69
    eliminating clutter, 90, 180
    explanation of, 11–12, 58
    "flow" state, 78
    fresh air, 91
    health screening, 159
    journals, 87
    meditation, 71, 105, 112, 126–27,
        131, 170
    mental health screening, 159
    morning routines, 49, 70, 174
    museum visits, 89
    music, 73, 76, 88, 101
    nature, 91, 129
    new experiences, 63, 81, 85, 89, 166,
        179, 182, 210

    organizing tips, 90, 180, 209
    phone breaks, 60, 92
    podcasts, 36, 65, 192, 215
    productivity tips, 59, 62, 78, 84, 170
    reading, 59, 61, 94
    red flags, 62, 144
    snacks, 21, 30, 95
    stress management, 64, 68, 72, 75,
        81–82, 86
    taking breaks, 60, 62, 84, 92
    working with hands, 82
    writing exercise, 67, 203
Mentors, 120, 148, 151
Mindfulness, 103, 117, 119, 135
Mistakes, learning from, 64, 66, 155
Money management, 193, 196
Morning Pages, 203
Museum visits, 89
Music, 73, 76, 88, 101

Nature, enjoying, 91, 129
Negativity, stopping, 66, 71, 75, 123, 130,
    145, 150, 162
Networking, 148, 197
New experiences, 63, 81, 85, 89, 166, 179,
    182, 210
Nostalgia, 161

Open mind, 116, 164, 210
Optimism, 164, 165, 175
Organization tips, 90, 180, 209

Personality test, 124, 204
Pets, 163

Physical self-care
  balancing body, 17–55
  beverages, 19, 22, 25, 39, 52
  clothing, 54
  doctor appointments, 43
  exercise, 24, 33, 36–40, 44, 46,
    50–51
  explanation of, 10–11, 18
  eye care, 41
  healthy foods, 21, 27, 30, 32, 42,
    47, 95
  hydration, 19, 52
  hygiene, 23, 45
  illnesses, 23, 43
  lungs, 37, 73, 91
  massage, 28
  posture, 31, 46
  sexual safety, 34
  skin care, 19, 35, 48, 53, 55, 112
  sleep/naps, 20, 26, 49, 157, 173
  substance abuse, 25, 37, 39
  sunscreen, 35, 55
  vitamins, 55, 80
Podcasts, 36, 65, 192, 215
Portfolio, 201, 202
Positivity, 147–48, 151, 160–61, 169, 174
Posture, 31, 46
Power naps, 26, 157, 173
Prayer, 99, 101, 108, 112, 123, 126–31
Procrastination, 74, 178
Productivity tips, 59, 62, 78, 84, 170
Professional self-care
  career counseling, 186, 202, 205
  career goals, 13–14, 121, 177–215
  computer coding, 200

credit cards, 193
curiosity, 210, 212, 215
documentaries, 212
elective classes, 69, 188
eliminating clutter, 90, 180
explanation of, 13–14, 178
financial aid, 65, 189
inspirational quotes, 87, 187, 214
internships, 54, 117, 140, 148, 178,
  185, 211
job shadowing, 199
leadership skills, 104, 190, 192, 194
life coaches, 205
money management, 193, 196
networking, 148, 197
new experiences, 179, 182, 210
open mind, 210
organizing tips, 90, 180, 209
part-time job, 183
personality test, 124, 204
personal statements, 207
podcasts, 36, 65, 192, 215
portfolio, 201, 202
professor relationship, 185
self-confidence, 54, 152, 157
seminars, 118, 208
student loans, 75, 167, 189, 195
study abroad programs, 85, 146,
  186, 198
study ritual, 181
switching majors, 213
tutors, 115, 143, 183, 206
vision boards, 187
volunteerism, 104, 106, 163, 190
writing exercise, 67, 203

Professors, relationship with, 185
Purpose, sense of, 13–14, 104, 121, 125, 178, 205
Puzzles, 72, 79

Questions, asking, 77, 118, 185
Quotes, 87, 187, 214

Reading tips, 59, 61, 94, 102
Red flags, 62, 144
Retreats, 105, 106
Rituals/routines
  bedtime routine, 20
  changing, 68
  evening ritual, 126
  exercise routine, 33, 46, 50
  morning routines, 49, 70, 174
  spiritual rituals, 126, 128
  study ritual, 181
Runs/walks, 36, 38, 44, 50–51, 62, 91

Safe sex, 34
Savings account, 193, 196
Saying no, 139, 154
Security, 122, 158, 173
Self-awareness, 168
Self-compassion, 157
Self-compliment, 142, 157
Self-confidence, 54, 152, 157
Self-criticism, 64, 142, 174, 203
Self-description, 152
Self-esteem, 31, 109, 142
Self-reflection, 105, 113, 126, 128
Seminars, 118, 208
Sexual safety, 34

Single life, 146
Skin care, 19, 35, 48, 53, 55, 112
Sleep/naps, 20, 26, 49, 157, 173
Smoking, 37
Snacks, healthy, 21, 30, 95
Social media breaks, 60, 92
Spiritual self-care
  acupuncture, 132
  advisors, 120
  alone time, 103, 113, 141, 149
  astrology, 133
  books, 102
  candles, 128
  causes, 100
  chakras, 109
  crystals, 130
  different religions, 110, 116, 118, 127, 131
  essential oils, 112
  evening ritual, 126
  explanation of, 12, 98
  faith history, 127
  friendships, 85, 116
  gardening, 134
  gratitude list, 107
  helping others, 100, 104, 125, 174
  highs and lows, 111
  hygge practice, 122
  interfaith events, 131
  mantras, 123, 174
  meditation, 71, 105, 112, 126–27, 131, 170
  mindfulness, 103, 117, 119, 135
  ministry retreat, 106
  nature, 91, 129
  nourishing spirit, 12, 97–135

open mind, 116
prayer, 99, 101, 108, 112, 123, 126–31
quiet moments, 113
retreats, 105, 106
rituals, 126, 128
self-reflection, 105, 113, 126, 128
sense of purpose, 104, 121, 125
stress management, 108–9, 115, 119,
    129, 132
sunrises/sunsets, 135
tarot cards, 114
values, 124
volunteerism, 104, 106
worship services, 99
Sports teams, 24, 146
Stress management
emotional self-care, 151, 153, 163,
    167–73
mental self-care, 64, 68, 72, 75,
    81–82, 86
spiritual self-care, 108–9, 115, 119,
    129, 132
Student loans, 75, 167, 189, 195
Study abroad programs, 85, 146,
    186, 198
Study breaks, 62, 84, 103, 126, 170
Study time, 59, 62, 68, 78, 84, 181
Substance abuse, 25, 37, 39
Sudoku, 79
Sunrises/sunsets, 135
Sunshine, 35, 55
Support systems, 143, 151, 158, 172

Tarot cards, 114
Tea/coffee, 19, 22, 52

Thank-you notes, 148
Time
alone time, 103, 113, 141, 149
blocks of, 59, 126
managing, 39, 74, 183, 194
study breaks, 62, 84, 103, 126, 170
study time, 59, 62, 68, 78, 84, 181
unstructured time, 103, 126, 170
Travel, 85, 146, 186, 198
Triggers, emotional, 156
Tutors, 115, 143, 183, 206

Values, determining, 124
Vision boards, 187
Vitamins, 55, 80
Volunteerism, 104, 106, 163, 190
Vulnerability, 81, 143, 155

Walks/runs, 36, 38, 44, 50–51, 62, 91
Water/hydration, 19, 52
Wellness programs, 33, 37, 39
Workouts, 33, 46, 93

Yoga, 20, 33, 70, 119

ABOUT THE AUTHOR

Julia Dellitt is a freelance writer whose work has been published by *BuzzFeed*, *Forbes*, Self.com, *Lifehacker*, *Brides*, *The Everygirl*, Aaptiv, and more. She graduated from the University of Chicago with a master's degree in religion and literature, and from Augustana College with a degree in English and political science. She lives with her husband and two children in Des Moines, Iowa. To find out more, visit julmarie.com.

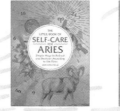